Anthony Pearson became a journalist 'accidentally' in Nairobi, Kenya, when he was sixteen. He trained as a reporter for the *East African Standard*, then went on to become an agency reporter, staff reporter for the *Guardian*, special foreign correspondent for the *Manchester Evening News* and a freelance war correspondent contributing to British, American and European newspapers and magazines.

He has covered the Middle East consistently since the Six-Day War of which the *Liberty* incident was an important part. During the October 1973 war, he reported for the Manchester *Evening News* from the fighting fronts of Israel, Syria and Egypt, the only reporter to cover the war in this single-handed way.

Over the past ten years he has become a specialist in terrorism and guerilla warfare, having had practical experience when covering what he calls 'street fire fight war'. He says, 'I am now more soldier than journalist'.

Anthony Pearson is thirty-seven years old and an inveterate wanderer, 'I live where I happen to drop that night'. His home is in Nairobi, Kenya.

CONSPIRACY OF SILENCE

Q_____

ANTHONY PEARSON

QUARTET BOOKS

LONDON MELBOURNE NEW YORK

First published by Quartet Books Limited 1978
A member of the Namara Group
27 Goodge Street, London W1P 1FD

Copyright © 1978 by Anthony Pearson

ISBN 0 7043 2164 5

Photoset, printed and bound
in Great Britain by
REDWOOD BURN LIMITED
Trowbridge & Esher

To My Mother and Father

CONTENTS

ILLUSTRATIONS

(between pages 88 and 89)

Chapter One

During the summer of 1975 I was broke. It was the worst broke I had ever been, although I tried not to give in to it and kept up appearances by moving into a new apartment in Cheyne Place, Chelsea.

Towards the end of the summer, it was in August I think, I was commissioned by Bob Guccione, the owner and publisher of *Penthouse* magazine, to research and write an article about the attack made on an American navy ship, the USS *Liberty*, by Israeli forces during the June war of 1967.

The commission was a chance thing. I had already been carrying the idea around for five months and had been unable to raise much interest in it. Most of the newspaper and magazine people to whom I showed the synopsis thought it a dead subject from a long-past history. When I explained that the incident had never been investigated by the press and that no attempt had been made by the Government of either Israel or the United States to offer a credible reason why the attack should have occurred, I was told it was best left as it was; it was best left forgotten.

At the time, because I was at a low ebb, I found it hard to write and harder still struggling to sell stories to uninterested ·and unsympathetic news editors. My column in the *Guardian* had been terminated a long time earlier and my work as a foreign reporter had come to a standstill. I still had occasional bursts of inspiration; I would produce long scenarios for stories and go out to sell them, full of enthusiasm, but would be blocked at every turn. The next day I would wake up disillusioned again.

The *Liberty* was not one of those sudden sensational ideas. That was mostly, I think, because I soon began to agree with the critics of the idea and when I met Guccione I had all but abandoned it as a useless antique.

I had been commissioned by the *Guardian* to write a feature on men's magazines. An interview with Bob Guccione was a part of this assignment. It began a short but interesting working relationship with a man I liked immediately and continued to admire even after our working and personal relationship disintegrated, in the aftermath to the publication of the *Liberty* article.

But whatever lay in the future, Guccione was responsible for launching the investigation and for publishing the article which was the forerunner to the story I am to tell, and he also played a small but important part in it.

Guccione did not have to think long and hard about it or argue the merits of its timing and historical significance. He said he thought it was a good story and if I could find the hidden reasons behind it, it might even be a great story. In the beginning he had more enthusiasm for it than I did. I guess this made him a better newsman than I was.

I had just moved into my new Chelsea apartment and the day of the Guccione commission I gave a party which went on all night. It was like the old days when I was a younger and a faster-moving foreign correspondent. The next day I began my investigation and the old depression returned. Time and time again I came up against a high blank wall: the beginning of something was suddenly cloaked in a shroud of silence and became nothing. The long slog of tramping London's streets to newspaper libraries, to government offices, to embassies, to the library at the British Museum; thumbing through page after page of books on the Six Day War was not just tedious – it almost destroyed my belief that I had the germ of a story and my conviction in my ability to tell it.

I had been a reporter since running away from school to Africa at the age of sixteen. I was now 34, still aimless, still rootless, still running. Now I was committed to a project which I felt frightened of because it was the only thread I had left to hold on to and it seemed likely to break at any moment and leave me with nothing.

Soon after I began my preliminary investigations I found my first major difficulty: working for *Penthouse*. There was no back-up, no news desk to coordinate information, no librarian to filter things back to me, no point of contact to provide a base when I began to travel. Most important of all, there was no reputation behind me.

When I worked for the *Guardian* and was foreign reporter for its subsidiary, the *Manchester Evening News,* I always had the strength of the paper behind me. Its reputation and authority opened doors. Working for *Penthouse,* this treatment acted in reverse. The name of the magazine was more likely to get doors slammed in your face. Even Bob Guccione advised me to work without telling anyone who had really commissioned the piece. So I was completely alone. It was the first time I had ever been so alone, even as a freelance writer. I think I only survived the first, most difficult hump of the investigation because of the help and support of my old friends at the *Guardian.* Each time I went into the office it was like coming in out of the cold. The feeling of normality there revived me.

Investigations like the *Liberty* affair are as much affairs of luck as of skill, and a long-shot inquiry I had made to a former colonial police friend who now worked for the Foreign Office one day produced a telephone call asking if I would like to meet over lunch to discuss my story. I accepted.

At lunch my friend proposed that we trade information. He knew I had the beginnings of a dossier on a political sabotage operation against the Government of Australia in which an American friend, the man who had first suggested the *Liberty* story to me, was one of the background figures. If I did not consider this kind of exchanging information morally or professionally unethical, I could trade the Australian dossier for a detailed background account of the *Liberty* incident which involved a former British Army intelligence officer, now serving in the Arabian Gulf.

I did not pause to consider ethics. In the real business of journalism, they rarely carry any weight. I agreed to the trade.

My friend then gave me some ideas on basic lines of inquiry and I flew to Washington to follow them up, returning to London in mid-December.

Just before Christmas I set off on another trip, this time to Nairobi to meet a Major McKenna who was on leave from his Gulf posting.

The first part of this story, which concerns the background to the 1967 Arab-Israeli war and the attack against the USS *Liberty,* is mostly drawn from what Major McKenna told me, supported by facts given to me in Washington and later in Israel and Egypt. It is

3

the story of some of the participants in the affair. They are members of the US Navy, many of them survivors of the *Liberty*'s crew, senior officers in the Pentagon, friends and interested parties in the Central Intelligence Agency, other writers and commentators on Middle East affairs, and some important former members of the administration of President Lyndon B. Johnson.

The second part of the story tells of my own involvement in the affair. It goes back to before my meeting with Guccione and continues up to the very moment of finishing this manuscript and, perhaps, beyond it.

So I now go to the very beginning of the beginning of the story; it is, so to speak, a preface, set in a corner of southern Arabia called the Radfan, during a small but vicious war in May 1967 which preceded the more important Arab-Israeli June war. It was one of the intelligence operations in the Radfan war which resulted in the discovery of events which built up into the Six Day War, and coincidentally drew together all the characters in this story directly and indirectly, including the ship herself and me as the reporter of it all.

It began towards the end of another hot morning in the desert. It was just before midday . . .

Chapter Two

On the road from Dhala to Taiz in the rocky desert of the Yemen below the high, empty plateaux of the Jebel Radfan there was, on 15 May 1967, an army camp surrounded by a heavy wire and sand-bagged perimeter defence, manned at short intervals by machine-gun posts. The soldiers in the camp belonged to X Company, 45 Marine Commando. It was their duty to guard and control a checkpoint between the British-protected sheikhdom of Lahej and the Yemeni Republic. They manned their post between daily raids by hill tribesmen supported by irregular guerilla units from Yemen armed with Russian semi-automatic assault rifles. The tribesmen usually came in groups of between 50 and 300 or more, but sometimes it was one man trying to get close enough to throw a grenade. The tribesmen were brave but had a healthy respect for the British soldiers. Any strange Arab who approached the checkpoint did so slowly, holding his hands deliberately in front of him to show he carried no weapons.

On the morning of 15 May an Arab made such an approach to the checkpoint. He was dressed in ragged khaki pants, a Bedouin burnous draped around his slight frame and tied in with an old Army webbing belt, and a plain dirty-white kaffiyah wrapped around his head in the turban style of the Radfan tribesmen.

The Arab stopped as he came under the sights of two crossfire light machine guns and only advanced when the sergeant of the guard indicated he should do so, waving him forward impatiently and shouting 'OK, Ali. Eemshi! Eemshi!'

The Arab approached the sergeant until he stood less than two feet away and then said clearly in clipped English:

'May I lower my hands now, sergeant?'

The sergeant blinked and looked at the brown, hawkish Arab face, set off by a stubbly-sided Kuwaiti beard.

The man, still holding his hands forward, spoke again. In clipped tones he gave the sergeant his rank, number and squadron attachment to a unit of the Special Air Service regiment.

The sergeant telephoned the details forward and in minutes a Land-Rover driven by a major raced across from the command post of Commando Camp.

The man in Arab clothes climbed into the passenger seat, pulled off his kaffiyah and shook his long matted hair free of the fine dust which covered it. The major shook his hand.

'I don't know where you've come from, Captain, but you look shagged out.'

'From Hodeida via Taiz. My communication link broke down so I had to come in the hard way,' the captain said.

'Coming in the hard way' seemed always to mark the end of this captain's assignments. Most of the jobs were like this one, working under cover inside the enemy depots. At other times he would work in uniform, leading patrols deep into the Radfan and on to the Jebel Plateau, into areas where white soldiers never penetrated the hill tribes. His orders on these occasions were to mark out possible outpost sites and communication links for future action if the British Army needed to invade the desert strongholds to contain the growing rebellion fomented by South Yemen and aimed at forcing the British out of their Red Sea base at Aden and establishing independence.

The politics of the war did not concern the captain. He was 26 years old and had been a professional soldier for seven years. For the last four, he had been a desert intelligence officer. He spoke perfectly-accented Gulf Arabic with the guttural emphasis of the southern Bedouin hill tribes. Since leaving public school in England he had lived through the last colonial days of British rule in Africa and Arabia and was obsessed with the romanticism of his role as a colonial adventurer. On missions like the one he had just completed, infiltrating the enemy bases of Taiz and Hodeida and the hill strongholds of the tribesmen, dressed as a Bedouin mercenary, his fair skin dyed almost indelibly with a brown stain, he revelled in the Kiplingesque character which he became, almost a relic of the days of the 'great game' along the Khyber Pass in the British India of the nineteenth century. The captain and many of his brother officers believed this was how Arabia should be for all time. They convinced themselves and each other that they fought the Arab

6

tribesmen with admiration and respect. They explained how they understood the Bedouin thing that when the war was over the former enemy became the loved friend. They thought it a good philosophy.

Driving back to base with a young Marine Commando lieutenant, the captain complained in a jokingly bravado way about the golliwogs of the hills. He thought he did this without malice. The political terrorists of Aden were another matter. He and the other Arabophiles of the Regiment despised them because they were political. They admired the hill tribesmen because they were not. Politics was an unworthy matter for warriors.

He talked to the Commando lieutenant for a while about this, then, overcome by the bouncing motion of the Land-Rover and the heat of the desert sun, he fell into an easy sleep, his head supported by his hands, his elbow leaning awkwardly on the window frame of the door.

Four hours later, dressed in a plain short-sleeved khaki shirt, clean pressed khaki linen pants and suede desert boots, his long hair washed and pushed back under a floppy khaki patrol hat, the captain stood around a map table with a brigadier, a colonel, three civilians in loose short-sleeved shirts, knee-length shorts, high socks and the ubiquitous tan desert boots, and a major wearing the fawn beret with the winged dagger insignia of the SAS. He was the commanding officer of the captain's unit.

'The FLOSY [Front for the Liberation of South Yemen] office is on the third floor of this apartment building.' The captain pointed to a cross on the map of Taiz township. He went on, pointing to a close adjoining cross: 'Here, barely a hundred yards away, is the Egyptian military headquarters. The FLOSY Chief, Abdullah Al Asnay, is in constant touch with senior Egyptian intelligence officers as well as with Vladimir Ivchenkov, the head of the local KGB, and various of his minions on the Russian military liaison team. Until a fortnight ago, Egyptian troop strength in Yemen had reached in excess of 50,000 with another 160 Russian advisers including pilots, communications people and missile technicians. Now there is an almighty row developing between President Abdullah Sallal, the Sovs and Nasser's boys over the withdrawal

7

of Gyppo troops and supplies back to Egypt. So far, the Sovs have airlifted almost 20,000 Egyptian troops out of Yemen, including all except half a brigade of paratroopers. The talk in Asnay's office and from pick-ups on KGB radio communications is that the Israeli Army has massed troops at strength supposed to be as much as fifteen brigades, including a full armoured corps, on the edge of the Golan plateau north and south of Lake Tiberias. The reports say they appear to be squaring up for an attack on Syria within the next forty-eight hours.

'Now, these reports have been kicking around in the Russian communication network for the past two weeks and they have been saying similar things about Israeli troop movements for the last three months. What seems to be so fishy about it right now is that, while the Russian link to the Gyppos is constantly churning out this alarmist information, the private KGB lines to Moscow are saying more or less the opposite: that the Israeli Army is not strongly mobilized on either the Syrian or the Egyptian front but that the Jews do have a rapid mobilization plan they can carry out in less than ten hours. In other words, the Russians believe the Israelis *are* going to make some sort of war but only if someone else makes the first move. The Russians seem to be priming the Egyptians to make that move – and that is not the style of the Sov army.

'This seems to affect our immediate situation in two ways. The Yemenis are going to stir up the hill tribes and give us more stick in the Radfan. Also, despite Asnay's denials that the NLF [National Liberation Front] hasn't got any teeth, it looks as though they are going to escalate the internal terrorist war in Aden, combined with increased Yemeni irregular-unit attacks against the 1st Paras in Sheikh Othaman. At the same time I think they will try to jockey FLOSY out of power with a bit of internecine killing – which we should encourage.'

One of the civilians stopped the captain. 'Is the information you have on the Egyptian-Russian withdrawal from Yemen the only supporting evidence you have that the Egyptians are responding to the Soviet allegations of an Israeli troop build-up?'

'Yes, sir. My orders were to appreciate South Yemen guerilla and terrorist strengths. My feeling on the other matter is that the

8

threat of an Israeli attack, if the Sovs take it seriously, and the Gyppos pulling out of Taiz and Hodeida in such numbers, will ease the pressure on our forward troops in the Radfan and make it easier for us to concentrate on Aden proper. I suppose if the Jews feel able to fight Nasser's lot they must be pretty confident, and if they go ahead, bloody good luck to them. The only other thing is that Asnay's mob are lashing out in all directions, accusing people of working for us and our cousins at the CIA. I only mention this because they are doing it much more than usual. I know those chaps are all paranoid about American intelligence but the gossip around and about in the bazaars and the camps of the more intelligent hill-tribe leaders is that the Americans have been up to something pretty big in the whole area, buying up information about the Russians, their equipment and the various small-time rulers and Yemeni politicians in their pay.'

'Outside your report in detail is there anything more relevant to the situation beyond the immediate military emergency?' one of the civilians asked the captain.

'No, sir,' he said. 'I have yet to produce my written report but that will be done by tomorrow. However, overall, my intelligence is related purely to the opposition's military dispositions in the Radfan and the terrorist build-up in Aden.'

The colonel in the group, who was the commanding officer of the headquarters military intelligence section, told the civilians that he had other small pieces of information which had filtered in about Egyptian troop withdrawals from Yemen. Also, civilian intelligence were in possession of a weight of Soviet material from their infiltration of the Russian communication networks which confirmed what the captain had reported.

The brigadier at the head of the table told the captain he could now be dismissed from the meeting. The captain saluted and left the high-ceilinged room by the french windows. He walked slowly across the veranda and on to the long green lawn which smelled fresh in the breeze from the sea. Although it was very hot, in the high nineties, the captain felt cool and relieved after many days in the desert. He did not think too carefully about the information he carried in his head other than the necessity to turn it into a typewritten report, something he would do that night. It was the

9

part of his job he hated most of all. But right now it was time for the beer he had craved for many days.

He crossed the lawn to the Mess where he found a friend from the Queen's Own Hussars who was travelling down to the Point. The captain rarely drank in the Officers' Mess at headquarters and, because of the secret nature of his work, he did not mix widely with the officers of Middle East Command outside his own regiment. Just before 5 p.m. his fellow-officer took him to the Crescent Hotel at Steamer Point. There he would have his cold beer in the bar with his friend, Stan Meagher of the London *Daily Express*.

As he left the Land-Rover in front of the steps leading to the entrance to the Crescent, he heard the distant double thud of an explosion from the direction of Maala where the British service families lived in a cantonment of new high-rise apartment blocks.

'It sounds like the bandits are having a go at a patrol down Grenade Alley,' the captain said to his friend. 'Good luck.' The Land-Rover accelerated in the direction of Maala.

The captain walked into the hotel. At that moment nothing was going to disturb the satisfaction of the long-awaited beer. But he realized that whatever turn events in the north would take, right now he had his own war to deal with.

On the day the captain came out of the desert, an American ship was cruising slowly off the coast of Nigeria on the other side of the African continent. The ship was following a northerly course at a speed of 8 knots, some sixteen miles from the shore.

The ship carried the United States Navy identification number GTR5 marked in large white letters either side of the prow. It was the 450-foot USS *Liberty*, a converted World War II freighter now serving as a communications post and intelligence-gathering vessel, called in Navy slang a 'ferret'. She was a distinctive ship. Her superstructure was top-heavy with a complicated network of radio antennae and radar masts including a large dish-shaped revolving screen which was a sonar device known as 'the big ear'. Her own defence armaments were two stern and two forward mounted 50-calibre Browning machine guns. She had left her base at Norfolk, Virginia, in November 1966 to commence her fourth tour of duty as a ferret assigned to intelligence-gathering work in the southern

Atlantic. She was currently monitoring a political upheaval and army coup in Nigeria which was to lead in less than six weeks to the secession of the northern province of Biafra and to bloody war.

Liberty was on assignment to the National Security Agency which posted her information jointly for naval intelligence and the CIA. The information she was monitoring through her high radio masts was to be used later when the CIA assessed its position in the area before covertly supporting the breakaway Biafran government of General Ojukwu.

The operation of the ship was managed by two separate commands, although both were ultimately under the overall authority of its Captain, Commander William McGonagle. His deck officers and sailing crew comprised one command and amidships in the belly of the Liberty, inside a large custom-built area full of computers and radio receivers, were the members of the other command organized by an ex-Marine Corps major whose brief came from the NSA at Fort Meade. He and his men passed daily coded reports through a CIA listening station in Morocco to their American headquarters. Copies of reports were submitted variously in full or censored form to the White House, the Pentagon and the Central Intelligence Agency at Langley, Virginia.

Commander McGonagle was an experienced naval officer at 41 years of age. Tall, with a round good-looking cheerful face and short-cropped hair, he was a member of a large clannish family from Wichita, Kansas, and his appearance and his slow drawl stamped him firmly as a Midwesterner. Although quiet and often stern, he was both liked and respected by his officers and crew. He had a reputation at the Navy Department for total dependability in difficult situations and absolute discretion concerning the conditions, circumstances and results of his assignments. He was the perfect naval intelligence officer, and was fully experienced in the operation of ferrets.

In many ways, although a typical naval officer of his generation, the captain of this ship resembled more a figure from a Conrad epic. He had already been cut firmly in that mould through his work with this ship and with others. He was a veteran of Korea which was a desperate war, its naval engagements limited and small, but bloody and intense, all of which proves that Commander

McGonagle was familiar with the practice and techniques of combat. His command was not the finest or the most satisfying even to a commander in years of peace, policies of non-confrontation and declining naval powers. Twenty-three years earlier, McGonagle might have commanded a cruiser. Now he had to make do with a twenty-year-old converted civilian freighter and be glad of that command.

McGonagle's first officer, Lieutenant-Commander Philip Armstrong, of Norfolk, Virginia, was a much more openly cheerful and easy-going young man. Half of him was devoted to the Navy, the other half to his wife and five children back home in Virginia. At 32, Armstrong was very much the family man. While the younger officers constantly complained about the long periods of sea duty without port calls, the tedium never bothered Armstrong. He checked off each day as bringing him nearer home. He was always being teased about this by the younger lieutenants like Jim O'Connor, Stephen Toth, Maurice Bennet and Jim Ennis.

By mid-May *Liberty* was nearing the end of her duty run and was due to leave station to make a routine call and fuelling stop at Rota, Spain, at the end of the month. There she would receive new sealed orders which McGonagle confidently expected would dispatch the ship back to base.

Satisfied with the results of their monitoring work off the Nigerian coast, the *Liberty*'s crew were looking forward to going home. But there was still much work to be done and the ship was operating through full twenty-four-hour periods, unconcerned about the shaping of events in other places. It was not until 24 May that orders were received to sail with all possible haste for Rota. Since this required Commander McGonagle to pull his ship off station only a week before he was due to leave anyway, he was not greatly alarmed by the order. He would receive his sealed instructions at Rota. Like the good officer he was, he did not question or think about the early requisition of his ship. He did not speculate on her assignment once she reached the NATO base in Spain. Everyone else said that for sure she would be going home.

Chapter Three

Two days before *Liberty* received her reassignment orders and seven days after the SAS captain came out of the Radfan, President Abdul Gamal Nasser of Egypt threw a naval blockade across the Straits of Tiran. This sea passage formed the entrance to the Gulf of Aqaba in the Red Sea. Access through the Straits into the Gulf was economically and strategically essential to Israel, since at the nothern end of the Gulf lay the port of Eilat.

Nasser's decision to impose the blockade was a direct result of the Syrian alarm that the SAS captain had reported to the British intelligence authorities. In turn, they had passed this and other related information on to the CIA.

The events surrounding the supposed troop movements which were to lead directly to a confrontation with Israel had reached their final stages on 13 May when the Egyptian Defence Minister, Marshal Amer, received a message from his Syrian opposite number Hafiz Al Assad (now President of Syria) that reports had filtered into Damascus claiming eleven to thirteen Israeli brigades were massing against the Syrian positions along the Golan. An attack against Syrian army outposts on the Heights was planned for the night of 16/17 May between 4 and 5 a.m.

Egyptian intelligence had no immediate confirmation of any such troop movements when they were asked by Marshal Amer. But within hours of the request Sami Sheraf, Director of the President's office of information and Nasser's personal intelligence adviser (and secret head of the Egyptian staff of the Soviet KGB), personally confirmed that the reports were true. The Israelis were massing troops, he said, and Egypt needed to act in support of Syria by moving men to confront the Israeli Army in Sinai as a feint to draw the enemy from the Golan front.

The previous day, Friday, 12 May, Israeli Premier Levi Eshkol had made a statement condemning continued Palestinian guerilla activity across the Golan. He had threatened military operations against the Syrian frontier if these raids were not contained. Commentators had concluded that Eshkol's threat was based on the presumption that Egypt could not fight in support of Syria because it had too many armed units bogged down in Yemen. They were unaware that Nasser had already started to withdraw his soldiers from Yemen in order to support the garrisons in southern Sinai.

Later that day Eshkol made a statement to a closed meeting of Mapai Party leaders at the Yahdav club in Tel Aviv in which he again referred to making raids across the Syrian border to stamp out sabotage activities by Palestinian Fedayeen. But this time he made it clear that any such raids were not designed to encourage a direct confrontation with the Syrian Army. In the past month there had been fourteen cross-border raids by Fedayeen into Israel, and after considering its position the Israeli Government had issued authority for the army to 'pacify' the Syrian side of the border. Neither Eshkol nor any other Israeli leader made any statement even suggesting they wished to subvert or overthrow the Syrian Government by force.

The Egyptian naval blockade was supported by extensive troop movements on land. The army had deployed seven divisions into the Sinai Desert including two fully armoured divisions, numbering in total 100,000 men in Sinai and the Gaza Strip. This left Nasser with less than 50,000 men in reserve. The total mobilized strength of the Egyptian Army was 180,000 men, and there were still in excess of 30,000 remaining in Yemen even after the withdrawals were made. To support the infantry there were 806 tanks of the two armoured divisions, spread as equally as possible through the five infantry divisions. Nasser had committed himself totally to a confrontation to prevent what he believed was a plan to invade Syria. But by the time the naval blockade had been imposed, the invasion story had already worn thin.

On the surface Nasser's reaction to the Syrian threat seemed natural enough. Egypt was tied to that country as the United Arab Republic. But Nasser's generals had warned him that his Army was technologically inept, still too dependent on its Russian advisers who would take no part in an actual war, and generally in no shape to take on the Israeli Army alone.

For over a year the Russian KGB had been producing a steady

14

stream of reports about Israeli troop movements against Syria. These reports became so regular that most of the senior Egyptian officers simply ignored them. They continually stressed in their advice reports to Nasser that he must avoid confrontation until the Egyptian forces could master their new technological weapons, particularly the surface-to-air missiles. He was told to forget the Syrian alarmism altogether and to concentrate on stockpiling arms supplies and updating equipment to align Egypt with Israel militarily.

Nasser took little notice of his general staff. He preferred to listen to Sami Sheraf who constantly plugged the Soviet line Nasser wanted to hear and convinced the Egyptian President the Syrian threat had substance.

On 3 February 1967 the Russian newspaper *Izvestiya* had reported: 'War psychosis is mounting in the State of Israel. The country's armed forces are being alerted. All leave has been cancelled and all reservists are being called up. Large armed forces have been concentrated on the northern border.'

Following on this and other Soviet statements, almost as if there was a direct link between the incidents, the Palestinian commandos of Ahmed Shukeriy began to escalate their attacks from Syria and Gaza so that on 12 May a United Press International dispatch from Jerusalem reported that 'A highly placed Israeli source said today that if Syria continued a campaign of sabotage in Israel it would immediately provoke military action aimed at overthrowing the Syrian régime.'

It was this American agency dispatch fed to the UPI reporter through the US Embassy in Tel Aviv which was one of the first to contain any suggestion of Israel attempting to overthrow the Syrian Government. The Russians had made no such suggestions. Levi Eshkol continued to deny these allegations in a generally convincing way. He went so far as inviting the Soviet Ambassador, Mr Chuvakhin, to go the northern front to freely examine Israeli troop dispositions which, he said, barely reached one brigade strength. Mr Chuvakhin declined the invitation on the advice of the embassy KGB head.

The contradictions of the affair have never been resolved. Syrian intelligence had already handed a report to its Defence Minister

15

claiming that the American CIA in coordination with Israel and Jordan was planning 'a new Suez' to overthrow President Nasser and rid the area of the dual threat of Russian presence and Marxist/Arab nationalism. Assad passed this report on in memorandum form to the UN Security Council, adding the British in the plot for good measure, claiming that a defeat of Egypt would further 'colonial expansion in the Yemen'. He added that Britain had tried this manoeuvre once before and had failed when Prime Minister Anthony Eden, allied with France and Israel, threw his paratroopers against the Suez Canal in 1956.

The reasons the Syrians gave for implicating Jordan in the alleged plot were based on the supposed relationship King Hussein enjoyed with 'the Imperialists'.

Hussein represented the Hashemite monarchy hated by the nationalists; a Palestinian had shot his grandfather, King Abdullah, to death in the Al Aksa Mosque in Jerusalem in 1951. It was said Hussein was in the pay of the United States Government, a new agreement he established when he took power after his father's death and which resulted in his sacking the British General Sir John Bagot Glubb as Commander of the Arab Legion, expelling him from Jordan together with most of the Legion's other British officers. Two ex-Syrian Army officers, Colonel Hatoum and Major Badr Juma, who had been involved in an unsuccessful coup against the Baathist Government in Damascus in September the previous year, had fled to Amman where they were reportedly recruited as agents provocateurs by the CIA and added to the Syrian paranoia about Hussein. Major Juma had returned to Damascus and denounced the plot. He claimed that Colonel Hatoum, who as a paratroop brigade commander had put the left-wing Baathists in power in February 1966, was raising new opposition among the ultra left, pro-Chinese faction in the Syrian leadership to purge the Government and throw out the Russians.

Both the Syrians and the Egyptians went through May pointing to an American-Israeli Suez plot using wild stories like the Hatoum affair to support their case. Outside reaction claimed the allegations were the typical rantings of unstable nationalism. But picking through the threads of wild irrationality and propaganda it was possible to find some substance to the Arab claims.

The British who had lost a lot of face in the Arab world since the 1956 Suez débâcle still retained a good intelligence network in the Middle East. It had superior capability to the American operation which relied entirely on its liaison with the Israeli Mossad. The British Secret Intelligence Service (MI6) not only worked alone, relying entirely on the information of its own operatives, but still ran the structural network of Jordanian intelligence in much the same way as it had done during the time of British advisory control of the Arab Legion.

Reports coming in to the St James's, London, headquarters of MI6 from their agents and army desert intelligence officers suggested two apparently conflicting patterns in the approaching confrontation.

On one hand there certainly seemed to be the suggestion of a plan in progress instigated through the CIA to help Israel launch a limited offensive against Egypt. Agency cooperation reports to MI6 had admitted this in essence but not in detail. This was primarily aimed to secure Sinai as a defensible buffer between Egypt and Israel. It was also hoped to inflict a crushing military defeat on the Egyptian armed forces which would in turn lead to the discrediting of Nasser and his possible removal from power, probably by an army coup. On the other hand it was known through reports based on penetration of the KGB network in Yemen by the British, that while the Russians were aware that an American-Israeli plan existed, they were actually pushing Nasser into a warlike posture by constant alarms, the Syrian story in particular.

The KGB, like the CIA, knew the Egyptian Army was not in good enough shape to fight the Israelis and the Russians had no intention of providing Egypt with more than token materials and advisory help when the time came to fight. Moscow was not going to risk confrontation with America in the Middle East at this moment. Nasser was going to have to go it alone, and he was being led into trouble by the very people who should logically be warning him off it. It was at Sami Sheraf's urging that Nasser had ordered the blockade of the Straits of Tiran. If there had been any chance of his avoiding confrontation before 22 May, his decision on that day to take the blockade action sealed the fate of Egypt.

17

But it bothered western intelligence that the Russians were apparently leading Nasser into the trap which was first a military and then a political snare. The only logical explanation which could be constructed by piecing together the general Middle Eastern situation reports, Egypt's internal reports and an analysis of general Soviet long-term planning for the eastern Mediterranean area, was that the Russians also were anxious to get rid of Nasser.

The Egyptian President's public image still showed him to be a virulent critic of 'western imperialism', a rabidly anti-Zionist Arab nationalist and the strongest supporter of Soviet involvement with the Third World after Cuba's Fidel Castro. Although this was far from being a total façade, Nasser's pro-Soviet front was beginning to develop some cracks and flaws. He was dissatisfied with the extent of Soviet aid, both military and economic, which fell far short of his plans to improve the appalling poverty and social health of his country. For all his violent extrovert outbursts, Nasser was a true patriot. His policies had developed because he believed they were right for his country. By early 1967 he was convinced the Russians were not going to help him implement these policies unless they could be forced into escalating the amount of aid. Nasser had asked for increased aid and had been ignored by Moscow. Now he decided that if he opened a new chapter of diplomatic relations with Washington the threat of a change in Egyptian policy might push Moscow into increasing its aid support.

The KGB were furious with Nasser. The Russians did not like that sort of pressure and were not prepared to give in to it. There were other elements in the Egyptian Government more personally involved with Moscow and less idealistically inclined towards the future of Egypt than Nasser was. If Nasser fell from favour and then from power it would be easy for the Russians to replace him with a leader better disposed towards them. It was a policy they would continue throughout the Third World during the next ten years and which would become particularly evident in the war between Ethiopia and Somalia in the Horn of Africa in 1977-8.

British intelligence analysed the changing events in Egypt and the Russian attitude to it, and decided that when the KGB had read the CIA plan to depose Nasser they saw in it an opportunity to implement their own plans in Egypt without actually being responsible for the political upheaval there. The way things stood, the Americans and Israelis were going to do their job for them.

When this interesting hypothesis was submitted by MI6 to the CIA the response was cold. The Agency replied that this contention was impossible for many reasons. Their infiltration of Russian intelligence in the Middle East was deep, yet their agents had made no reports indicating the Russians were aware of any American-Israeli plans for the area.

MI6 was aware that all CIA operations in the Middle East were the responsibility of the Israeli Mossad and that Israel was not interested in Russian or American policies for Egypt. All the Israelis wanted was to capture new land to expand their settlements. War was the only way to do it and they were not going to pass any information to the Americans which might bring a halt to their coming war plans.

The closure of the Straits of Tiran sparked off both panic and protest in Israel, at the United Nations, in Britain and America. On 24 May, the day the USS *Liberty* received orders to travel from Nigeria to Rota, the Israeli Foreign Minister flew from Tel Aviv just after midnight.

It was early morning when Abba Eban reached Paris where Walter Eytan, the Israeli Ambassador, was waiting for him at Orly. Eytan told him a meeting with General de Gaulle had been arranged at very short notice.

De Gaulle was reserved with Eban but not unfriendly. But the moment Eban began to discuss the crisis, de Gaulle stiffened and became coldly aloof. He said he would do all he could to help bring about a settlement but this was not possible without consultation with the Soviet Union. A strong critic of the 1956 Suez operation, de Gaulle was not going to allow France to be caught up in any similar new adventure. He also told Eban that if he wished to put his trust in America that was his business; as for the blockade, France did not see this as necessarily a declaration of war. Eban told him that if there was a choice between surrender and resistance Israel would choose resistance, as de Gaulle had done in June 1940. The General was not impressed. De Gaulle was firmly convinced that a third world war was closer than most people

19

realized and if Israel started a shooting war in the Middle East the situation would become even more dangerous. Mr Eban was dismissed after forty-five minutes with a compliment on the quality of his French and a firm warning, as though he was a naughty schoolboy, that his country should behave itself and leave high-level strategic negotiations to the four major powers.

Disappointed, almost dejected, Eban flew on to London where he went directly to Downing Street. Prime Minister Harold Wilson gave him a little more encouragement but it did not amount to positive support. Wilson was angry about Nasser's interference with Israeli shipping and thought something should be done. But whatever action had to be taken should be done jointly by Britain and the United States. Wilson assured Eban that HM Government would take 'practical steps' if necessary, but he was not specific. Even though this was slightly more than Eban had expected, he left for Washington convinced that the only key to solving the crisis lay with the Americans.

Following his meeting with Eban, Harold Wilson called a session of Foreign Office and intelligence advisers to produce an assessment of the possibility of war in the Middle East and its implications. His principal concern was how it would affect the British security situation there, particularly as Nasser's blockade of the Straits of Tiran could be said to involve the British base in Aden, since Britain had committed strategic support to Israel as a member of NATO. Wilson was also concerned that an Arab-Israeli confrontation might develop into a confrontation between Russia and NATO, particularly as it was rumoured that the Israelis were in possession of a limited nuclear offensive potential.

So a request was transmitted to Aden for a reassessment of the current political situation and a fuller in-depth report on the military confrontation build-up in the Sinai Desert, with particular reference to any concentrations of missile sites which might indicate the presence of nuclear warheads to be used by the Israelis if things went badly for them.

On 27 May the SAS officer who had brought the news of Egyptian troop withdrawals from Yemen was dispatched to Cyprus with three other officers. They were to work on detached duty for MI6, and to travel to the imminent war areas to launch

20

penetration operations into the southern quarter of Sinai, along the Syrian border of Israel, and in Jordan and to 'appreciate the general military and political situation'.

They had flown from Aden to Nicosia and then split up to their individual assignments. The SAS captain was now on an El Al jet making its approach into Ben Gurion Airport, Tel Aviv. He was writing his details onto an immigration form. McKenna, Steven Vincent; Age: 28; Nationality: British; Place of Birth: United Kingdom; Permanent Domicile: United Kingdom; Profession: Researcher, British Central Office of Information.

After his arrival in Cyprus McKenna had been assigned to cover Israel. The other three officers had been assigned: one to Damascus, one to Amman and the third to Beirut and on to Cairo. Each operated under quasi British Civil Service cover. According to his papers, McKenna worked as a political affairs researcher of the Central Office of Information, Middle East Division.

McKenna passed quickly through Immigration, collected his suitcase from the baggage hall, checked through Customs and went out into the main hall of the airport to the Avis desk to collect the car he had reserved by phoning from the Ledra Palace Hotel in Nicosia. He had made his Tel Aviv hotel reservation at the Dan.

When he arrived, there was a note waiting for him from a 'Mr Clarkson' of the British Council. He had left a return telephone contact at the British Embassy. The note read: 'I received a call from Mr Hogg who asked me to take care of you during your stay in Israel. Please ring me at your earliest convenience.' Hogg was the *nom de guerre* of McKenna's civilian contact at MI6. He was the section chief of the Middle East Department, handling the details of the Arab-Israeli conflict and the work of Desert Intelligence Officer of the SAS on detachment to civilian intelligence. Clarkson's department, the British Council, was an overseas British Government-sponsored cultural organization which was often used to give cover to officers of MI6, in the same way as the CIA used the US Government's overseas welfare department, AID.

McKenna rang Clarkson immediately he got to his room, making a brief and simple arrangement to meet him at the Embassy at six. Clarkson also chatted briefly about characters at

21

the COI in London for the benefit of the tap there would be on McKenna's phone. McKenna answered his inquiries easily and cheerfully.

Promptly at six, McKenna arrived at the British Embassy. Over a large brandy and soda Clarkson told him that in February and March there had been meetings in Israel between groups of 'passing American civil servants' and senior Israelis, government people, politicians and members of the IDF general staff. These included Moshe Dayan, Yigal Allon, Shimon Peres, David Hacohen, Ezer Weizman, Aharan Yariv (head of military intelligence), Meir Amit (chief of combined intelligence), and Tzvi Zamir (head of the Secret Intelligence Service, Mossad). Clarkson remarked that they represented a regrouping of the old guard of the Palestine Emergency of the post-war British Mandate days. They were all former members of the Hagganah, the Palmach and the Irgun.

There had also been return visits by members of the Israeli team to Washington. Accompanied by the deputy Israeli Ambassador, Ephraim Evron, they had met with State Department people, defence chiefs and heads of the NSA and the CIA. They had discussed a limited operation in the Sinai Peninsula aimed at inflicting a significant defeat on the Egyptian Army. This operation was to be carried out by the IDF without any overt or covert aid from the United States. It was to be a repeat of the 1956 Suez operation but this time if it went wrong the Israelis were going to have to stand the blame alone. It was a brief résumé of the plan already presented in detail to the Foreign Secretary, the Ministry of Defence and the Prime Minister.

Both the NSA and the Pentagon had calculated that in open confrontation Israel would easily defeat the Egyptian forces. Their intelligence assessment of Egyptian internal feeling was that a defeat of the Egyptian Army by Israel would create a backlash of resentment against President Nasser from both inside and outside the army. There were many senior officers on the Egyptian General Staff who were deeply suspicious of Nasser's social reforms and Marxist-Nationalist politics.

There were other, deeper aspects of the plan which involved the growing Russia–NATO power struggle in the area but, McKenna was told by Clarkson, these did not concern him and were irrelevant to his immediate assignment which was to 'appreciate the situation' with particular emphasis on certain geographical areas. This involved making, as far as possible, a military survey into the movement of troops and equipment to points around Kiryat Gat, Bet Shaan, Ashkalon and Nitzana and to pay particular attention to activity in the Negev Desert between Ramon and Eilat, an empty quarter bordered on the east by Jordan and on the west by Sinai. It was a quarter where the Israelis maintained their top secret military installations. These included, Clarkson said, two nuclear processing plants and at least four missile ranges capable of launching long range ballistics with a possible nuclear capability.

Meanwhile Eban had arrived in Washington where he had to wait for more than twenty-four hours before he could meet President Lyndon Johnson. America had already launched an exercise code-named 'Operation Regatta' to break the Tiran Straits blockade. So far it had been confined to ineffectual diplomatic pressure and had proved a dismal failure. Nasser had gone too far to be turned back by simple diplomatic pressure. There was an added domestic problem, caused by the many different approaches to the crisis that various Washington government departments and agencies applied. The splits flawed and weakened the US diplomatic initiative but the overall strength of the powerful Jewish lobby in the Government left America's impartial status in severe doubt.

The President and his advisers were in favour of helping Israel. But many congressmen, for all their sympathy towards Israel were reluctant to see a heavy American commitment. They claimed it would develop into a second Vietnam. They were being realistic. On the other hand, the CIA were more sympathetic, working covertly where they could not afford to be seen openly. The White House was not aware of the deep historical reasons behind the Agency's sympathetic association with Israel. But it did know that the CIA's estimate of Israeli military prowess was high. According to intelligence reports, Israel could win a war not only against Egypt, but against any alliance of Arab states.

Eban's meeting with Johnson was arranged by Ephraim 'Eppy' Evron. Abba Eban attended the White House accompanied by Avraham Harman, the Israeli Ambassador.

23

Johnson was flustered. He had just received a communication from the NSA informing him that Israel was about to attack Egypt and the strike was coming a good deal sooner than the Americans had anticipated. Immediately the meeting began, Eban told Johnson that Egypt was about to attack Israel. Johnson tried to assure Eban that this was not the case, that America was escalating 'Operation Regatta' and the blockade of the Straits of Tiran would be broken within a few days. Beyond this, Johnson was unable to think of anything to tell the Israeli Foreign Minister. Throughout the meeting, which lasted barely half an hour, he fidgeted and looked for ways to get rid of the Israeli delegation so he could set his advisers to work on a more convincing story. He was also angry because Eban's mission seemed to be planned to dupe the United States into a false sense of security or else a false assessment of the situation. The real farce was that neither Johnson nor Eban had been briefed by their respective intelligence networks on the American/Israeli War plan.

Disgusted, Eban returned to Tel Aviv, reaching there on the evening of 27 May. He reported immediately to Prime Minister Eshkol. The Prime Minister was scarcely less than shocked by the results. He was already under severe pressure and there was talk of replacing him with a more suitable candidate, namely War Minister Moshe Dayan. Without hesitation, Eshkol went into a hastily convened meeting and placed the entire blame on Eban for the talks' failure. He was just as ignorant as Eban and Johnson. Nobody had made him privy to the war plan.

In Washington Eban's visit had caused consternation and confusion both in the White House and in the State Department. They were now fully aware from intelligence reports released after Eban's visit that the CIA had been involved in a covert plan with Israel to promote a war against Egypt and thus overthrow President Nasser. Now that war was looming darkly, but ahead of schedule and seemingly out of American control. The Secretary of State, Dean Rusk, decided there should be a quick about-face and an attempt should be made to try and placate Nasser by opening a new and more cordial relationship with Egypt. If this was done and the blockade of the Tiran Straits raised, there would be no excuse for the Israelis to attack Egypt. Rusk told a meeting of the Senate

Foreign Relations Committee that little could be done to force the blockade of the Tiran Straits at once because the United States had been compelled to limit her aims in organizing resistance to it. But this was not America's fault; it was because the other maritime nations, principally Britain, would not take a firm stand on the question of free passage through the international waterway.

Rusk was very intent on pushing Britain to the forefront to take the blame for the failure of the four powers to prevent a Middle East crisis. He did this on the direction of the White House. Johnson had told him that if a war could not be prevented the State Department should blame Harold Wilson for the crisis getting out of hand. It would be good strategy to switch the responsibility for selling Israel short onto Britain. Whatever happened, no one must find out that the whole mess was a result of meddling by the CIA. Whether the Agency had acted with or without the approval of the White House was irrelevant, the American Government would still have to take the blame.

On 1 June Dean Rusk saw the Egyptian Ambassador in Washington, while at the same time Foy Cohler and Eugene Rostow, both Under Secretaries of State, had a long meeting with the Russian chargé d'affaires. Johnson was playing the Soviets with kid gloves on.

Links were established by the Egyptian Ambassador with Cairo, and it was decided to order Charles Yost, a former American Ambassador to Damascus, who was currently in Cairo 'studying the situation', to see Nasser. Nasser refused to see him, saying he was too busy. But later that day after a meeting with his general staff he relented. However, he did not see Yost but Robert Anderson, a former Secretary of the Treasury, who was also in Cairo on the same diplomatic mission. The meeting was inconclusive. President Johnson had sent a personal message to Nasser on 30 May asking that talks be opened to seek a peaceful solution to the mounting problem. Nasser discussed this possibility with Anderson. On 3 June the American delegation returned home carrying a message from Nasser saying he would welcome a proposed visit by the American Vice-President, Hubert Humphrey, to Cairo and that he would send the Egyptian Vice-President, Zakaria Mohieddin, to Washington; but he did not fix a firm date for the exchange.

This message, which was released to the press for public consumption, was only a very small result of the talks. While Anderson was with Nasser, Charles Yost had met the Egyptian Foreign Minister in secret. They had concluded an agreement in principle that diplomatic channels should remain open and that Egypt would not raise objections to the question of the Tiran Straits being put before the International Court of Justice in The Hague. Mohieddin's visit to Washington would be more than a diplomatic exchange for Humphrey. He was prepared to go to the State Department and negotiate a compromise. In return for its cooperation Egypt was assured by the Americans that so long as diplomatic channels remained open, Israel would be prevented by the US Government from launching an attack against the Arabs. Later the Americans would be prepared to discuss a whole new pact with Egypt which could provide Nasser with the financial aid he needed to promote his social reforms and phase out the heavy interference of Russia.

On 2 June Johnson conferred with Harold Wilson in Washington and, although much was said publicly about ending the Middle East crisis, the strength of the four powers and the power of the UN Security Council, nothing was concluded.

Wilson had proposed what he called a 'safeguard solution' for Johnson. This was to allow Nasser to keep the territory he had gained, that is, to occupy territory held by the United Nations peace-keeping force, in return for written guarantees allowing for the unopposed existence of the Israeli State as it stood. Johnson told the British Premier this idea could not be supported by the United States as it would bring too much criticism 'from the Jewish community and the friends of Israel' in America. Such a plan would also imply America was giving way, even though only indirectly, to Russian pressure, and in view of the strong anti-Communist stand of the administration over Vietnam, to back down on a Soviet confrontation side-issue was unthinkable.

Without any of the principals able to agree on strong unified action, the situation dragged on until the early hours of 5 June. At midnight Washington time, 7.00 a.m. Middle East time, squadrons of the Israeli Air Force numbering almost 320 combat planes, half of them bombers or fighter-bombers, took off from their bases and headed south-west across the Sinai Desert. Covered by the early morning mist over the Suez Canal, they hit every Egyptian airfield simultaneously, destroying 286 of Egypt's 340 aircraft. Flying low behind the Sinai mountains to beat the Egyptian radar and anti-aircraft missiles or sweeping in from the sea, the Israeli aircraft took the Egyptians completely by surprise. The first attack was timed when the Egyptian pilots were relaxing on the ground after returning from their dawn patrols. Only a handful managed to scramble their MiG fighters and offer token resistance. All of them were shot down.

At 8.15 a.m. Tel Aviv time, headquarters IDF southern command gave the order to attack the Egyptian ground forces.

The suddenness of the Israeli strike almost took the Americans by surprise, but not altogether. Intelligence reports released at the time of the Eban visit forecast a war 'by 10 June'. The Israelis pre-empted them by five days. When Abba Eban left Washington on 27 May, Johnson's conference with the intelligence chiefs resulted in the rapid formation of a contingency plan to prevent a local Middle East war spilling over into a Russian–NATO confrontation and a possible escalation into world war. One of the problems which constantly dogged the Pentagon and the NSA was the knowledge that Israel possessed (albeit secretly) ballistic missiles capable of carrying nuclear warheads. They were also aware that after the 1956 Suez crisis, when President Eisenhower had forced Israel to abandon captured territory in Sinai with threats of force if that force was necessary, elements in the CIA led by James Angleton had given the Israelis technicians and probably even material to set up their own nuclear plants and projects. This had been done, partly as a sop to temper Eisenhower's demands over Sinai, and also to facilitate a very necessary liaison between the rapidly developing Israeli intelligence service and the CIA. The liaison was based on an agreement, already referred to, that Mossad would handle all CIA operations in the Middle East and that there would therefore be very little actual presence of Agency personnel.

The American fear was that since Israel was prepared to go to war over the head of Washington, the Israeli war commitment would be total, and despite the confidence of the Pentagon that they would win, there was still the unforeseen in the shape of Arab/Russian missile complexes, a capability which had not been tested although these were conventional, not nuclear. If these missiles were used to turn the war against the Israelis or to attack Israeli cities, then it was highly probable that the Israelis would respond by firing nuclear missiles at Damascus and Cairo. If this happened the Russians would probably respond in kind against Israel. Anxious that they should be clear of any responsibility if nuclear weapons were used, the State Department expressed these fears to the Soviets at meetings in Washington. The Russians were understanding and cordial and it was agreed each side should contain its wards to prevent widescale confrontation if this became a real threat. But the cordiality was superficial. Neither side was prepared to discuss its military contingency plans in the eastern Mediterranean, particularly the deployment of their respective navies.

American naval intelligence already knew that the Russians had at least six intelligence ships in the eastern Mediterranean working with two Echo-class conventionally-powered submarines armed with long-range missiles with nuclear warhead capability. America in turn had two Polaris nuclear-powered submarines operating with the Sixth Fleet; it was decided to increase this strength by one more to work covertly outside the normal range of the Sixth Fleet close to the battle area. *So that this submarine could be kept informed with a minute-by-minute relay of the movement of events she would need to work closely with an intelligence communications monitor ship.* The NSA informed the Pentagon and the White House that it had already ordered a naval ferret to make port in the NATO base at Rota. There she would rendezvous with the USS *Andrew Jackson,* a Polaris submarine, out of base at Holy Loch in Scotland. The order the deployment of these ships was approved by the Joint Chiefs of Staff and the necessary arrangements were made to equip them and move them to a station off the Sinai Peninsula as soon as possible.

Chapter Four

On 29 May the USS *Liberty* arrived at Rota. There she made rapid provision for a full four weeks' tour of duty, taking on extra fuel and supplies and exchanging the African Hausa and Ibo linguists in the Communications Room for Arabic- and Hebrew-speakers. The commander of the Communications Room was also relieved. The new man, known only to the crew as 'the Major', was an NSA official registered by the Pentagon as 'a civilian', Allen M. Blue.

The *Liberty* sailed from Rota on 2 June. She had orders to hasten with all possible speed to an operational area designated as 'north of the Sinai Peninsula'. She carried a full crew complement of 15 officers, 279 men and three listed Department of Defence technicians.

One day later the *Andrew Jackson*, now on covert attachment to the US Sixth Fleet, sailed with posted orders taking her to the same location and with special verbal orders not to break radio silence except in the case of a Red One alert. The submarine commander was also ordered not to abort his mission unless directly instructed to do so by the White House.

Acting jointly as a liaison with the *Andrew Jackson* and as a surface intelligence-gathering machine made *Liberty*'s mission doubly dangerous, a fact of which Commander McGonagle was well aware. During his career serving in South-East Asia principally as an intelligence officer on ships similar to the *Liberty*, he had observed and experienced the many difficulties, small mistakes, or moments of plain bad luck which could expose a covert operation and lead to its collapse and failure, often followed by disaster. Friends of McGonagle from the Defence Intelligence Agency (DIA) had been on two US destroyers which were torpedoed in the Gulf of Tonkin in the summer of 1964 after their clandestine intelligence-gathering mission had been discovered by the North Koreans who retaliated by launching an attack with motor torpedo boats. Ever since then McGonagle had thought long and hard about the vulnerability of his and other ships attached to the naval intelligence branch of the NSA. Orders were to bluff and not fight your way out of a tight situation if possible. The communications equipment effectively cut down the fighting capabilities of an intelligence ship. *Liberty* had only her four 50-calibre Brownings. Against an aggressive attack pressed seriously they were of little use. In the event of such an attack McGonagle realized he had to accept that no quarter would be given. An attack against any vessel operating in secret would have to be itself kept a closely guarded secret if political response was to be suppressed. Such an attack would aim to wipe a spy ship off the face of the ocean and kill every member of the crew.

The other alternative would be to board and capture for a political show trial. Commander McGonagle had determined he would never be disgraced in this way. If his command went, it would be to the bottom of the sea without leaving a single man or piece of equipment the enemy could use to their advantage.

Liberty made a fast passage along the direct North African coastline route to Gaza and arrived off station by midday on 5 June.

During the first forty-eight hours of her mission the ship remained well out of striking range of the Egyptian coastline. But shortly after midnight on 8 June a communication was received asking the ship to move closer inshore.

When it was passed from the Communications Room to Commander McGonagle, the captain allowed himself to speculate on why the NSA and the Pentagon wished him to take his ship into an area which made him so highly vulnerable to attack.

Although his ship had been involved in the last three days in transmitting continuous batches of war information, its primary role was still as a liaison with *Andrew Jackson*. McGonagle noted that the submarine had also been ordered to move closer inshore.

When the Arab-Israeli war began the listening devices on *Liberty* had been tuned to transmissions from both sides. With radar monitoring it had been possible to carefully map the movements and positions of troops, armour and aircraft showing the true progress of·battle. This information was being transmitted in full to the NSA at Fort Meade and selected parts were being passed to the UN Security Council in New York.

It had quickly become clear to the observers on *Liberty* that the strength of the Israeli offensive lay in a superb intelligence capability. The Israelis had broken the Arab codes from the moment the fighting began and were tuned to every Arab communication. The importance of this became evident when the *Liberty* began monitoring exchanges of war information between Nasser and King Hussein of Jordan concerning the strategy and progress of the Arab allies. Somewhere between Cairo and Amman in a field relay station hastily constructed in Sinai, the messages were being blocked by the Israelis, reconstructed and passed on so swiftly and effectively that there was no apparent break. The outgoing transmissions from Egypt did not appear in the same form as incoming transmissions to Jordan. In the language of electronic intelligence this type of interference is called 'cooking'.

The first batch of these messages transmitted from Cairo advised King Hussein of the bad military situation in Sinai, that the Egyptian Army was hard pressed and was unable to give him tactical support to hold his position on the West Bank. The message also told Hussein that the Israelis now had total air superiority and that he could expect heavy airstrikes against his ground troops with no chance for the Arab armies to throw any opposition against them. The Israelis blocked these transmissions and re-worded them to misinform Hussein that three-quarters of the Israeli Air Force had been destroyed over Cairo and the 300-plus aircraft he was now picking up on radar approaching Jordan were Egyptian jets sent to raid targets in Israel. They were in fact Israeli aircraft returning from the destruction of Egyptian airfields.

Throughout the first day of fighting the Israelis continued to cook the Arab transmissions to give both the Egyptians and the Jordanians an impression the war was going favourably for the Arabs. There was no chance for the plan to go wrong because Hussein had broken off diplomatic relations with Syria over allegations of sabotage by the Syrian Secret Service a week before the Israeli attack, and so he was not in communication with Damascus. No Israeli interference with messages between Cairo and Damascus was necessary because the Syrians, although

31

apprised of the bad situation in Sinai, were also being told by the Egyptians that their flank was still covered by the Jordanian Army. This encouraged them to withdraw troops from the Golan towards Damascus in order to provide a second line of defence over the road from Amman when the Jordanian Arab Legion launched an expected counter-attack against Israeli positions in Hebron. The Egyptians had been misled by the Israeli cooking on 6 and 7 June into believing that the Jordanians were making this successful attack in Hebron and they in turn counter-attacked during the early hours of 8 June, ignoring a United Nations call for a cease-fire which would have greatly limited the extent of the final Arab defeat. As they launched their counter offensive the Egyptians marched into a carefully-laid Israeli pincer ambush and were badly mauled and forced to retreat, losing all their heavy equipment. McGonagle believed it was this alarm which had caused the NSA to order *Liberty* and *Andrew Jackson* to take a new position as close inshore off the Sinai Peninsula as it was possible to go. As dawn broke on 8 June *Liberty* stood thirteen miles off the coast of Gaza directly out from the town of Al Arish.

The Officer of the Watch was 27-year-old Lieutenant Stephen Toth. His father was a retired captain whose last years of service had been in naval intelligence. His son had followed him into the same corps. Lieutenant Toth noted in the log that the day was still, the sea calm and the sky clear. He had been on watch most of the night and he had seen the dawn break in a golden purple hue which indicated a long spell of fine weather. There were no streaks of horse-tail cirrus cloud in the sky to indicate any wind. What little cloud there was hung high, white and fluffy. *Liberty* had been steaming at a steady 8 knots through the night. There had been a smooth regular phosphorescence from her engine wake, steady and reassuring like the regular beat of her diesels, which disappeared with the sun's rising.

As the light and visibility increased Toth was able to see first the outline of the Sinai coast and then the detail. Inland a little, but not more than two miles, he observed three columns of black smoke rising straight and high, almost perpendicular because there was no wind. He could also see the minarets of the mosque at Al Arish which seemed to stand equidistantly between two of the columns of smoke and just in front of the third column as if the mosque had been a point of zero targeting for the device which had started the fires from which the smoke arose.

Toth was aware, as all the ship's personnel were, that the war in progress in Sinai was now in full favour of Israel. They did not all know what form the war had taken that morning along this Gaza coastline. But the smoke columns hung ominously. There was an awful, sinister element in the barely wavering straightness of the black smoke. The fact of the smoke was noted in *Liberty*'s log. Apart from it, there was no sight or sound of war and the morning was as peaceful as the sea which was only disturbed on the desert shore where a slight surf broke along the sand.

Despite the overall sense of solitude and calm, Commander McGonagle was uneasy; he had placed *Liberty* in a 'modified condition of readiness three'. This was a normal operational state when the ship was on station and not simply moving between posts. It meant a regular steaming watch. An officer and non-commissioned officer were stationed on the bridge, one seaman manned the forward machine guns and a standing-watch was on call to operate the after guns in the event of an emergency.

The speed of the ship at readiness three was between 6 and 10 knots, depending on sea conditions. On this day the *Liberty* was maintaining her night cruising speed of 8 knots.

Between first light and breakfast nothing much happened. The officers, petty officers and seamen rose, washed and dressed at 7 a.m. and ate breakfast at 7.30. The atmosphere in the wardroom and on the mess desk was happy and relaxed in keeping with the warm sunshine and the calm sea. Later on in the day officers and men not on watch would hope to stretch out on the lee decking in order to add to their Mediterranean tan.

After breakfast the crew fell to regular morning maintenance duty and took station for the early day watches.

At 8.50 a.m. the *Liberty* reached a point about 28 miles due north-west of Tel Aviv. Captain McGonagle then ordered his ship turned on a south-westerly course, making a sweep inshore along the Gaza coast exactly as they had done through the night.

As *Liberty* made the turn to course a single unidentified jet aircraft, easily sighted because of the long white conn-stream it trailed, crossed her wake between three and five miles astern. In the clear conditions and at cruising speed it was difficult to assess exactly how far away the aircraft was. No signal was made to the ship from the plane or to the plane from the ship. Captain McGonagle went to the bridge and saw the aircraft for himself with his number one, Lieutenant-Commander Armstrong. The jet could be a Russian or Arab MiG, an American A4 Skyhawk, a British Buccaneer from Akrotiri, Cyprus or an Israeli Mirage or Mystère. Its presence was noted in the log but the readiness condition and the course of the ship remained undisturbed.

For the next two hours work on the ship carried on as usual. Deck operations were finished and *Liberty* continued to cruise parallel to the Gaza coast, but now moving at a speed of no more than 5 knots, to allow for careful radio monitoring inside the lower-deck Communications Room. This was fitted exactly as it had been off Nigeria with normal radio-communication equipment, high-powered units with a variable contact distance up to 1,500 miles and computerized signals-analysis gear which allowed monitored coded communications to be broken down. These were analysed, decoded and translated, then the intelligence they contained was transmitted to Fort Meade. Final transmissions would be in US or NATO code, depending on the information in the signal. But nothing in the ship's log or even in her incident reports mentioned the function of the equipment or even that it was carried. It was only noted officially that the *Liberty* had 'an extensive communications area'.

At 10.56 a.m. two jet aircraft circled the ship at a distance of two miles or so and a height of between three and four thousand feet. Another hour passed. At 11.26 a.m. the two jets again circled the ship at the same careful distance. This time they were joined by a propeller aircraft. Lieutenant-Commander Armstrong took the planes under observation with his glasses. They were too far and too high for him to identify their type or their markings.

After circling *Liberty* for about five minutes, the planes banked and flew away in an east-south-easterly direction. Lieutenant-Commander Armstrong queried the presence of the aircraft to Commander McGonagle but the ship's captain suggested that the activities of the aerial surveillance should in no way interfere with the *Liberty*'s operation and also that if the position, speed and direction of the ship had been noted the logical thing to do was to maintain them so as not to arouse suspicion. *Liberty* was marked with her Navy identification number on either bow and flew a standard ensign of 5' X 8' from the masthead. Her presence in the area was not official. But neither was the presence of two Russian 'trawlers' they had sighted the previous day. Movement orders for the Sixth Fleet to enter the eastern Mediterranean in a condition of 'readiness Red One' had not yet been issued. But McGonagle had received a signal warning him that the Russian battle-cruiser *Moskva* had been ordered to detach from the Soviet Black Sea Fleet and make her way through the Bosporus Straits to the eastern Mediterranean.

After the second sighting and logging of aircraft during the morning, the officers went down to the wardroom to take a coffee break. Sitting around easy and relaxed, the portholes open to take in the little breeze, they discussed the behaviour of the aircraft. Lieutenant Toth and the ship's doctor, 34-year-old Lieutenant Richard Kiepfer from Brooklyn, New York, decided that the behaviour of the aircraft was both sinister and of some concern. Commander McGonagle shrugged their fears aside. He told them that whatever the motive for the surveillance, the implications were not necessarily aggressive. He had decided that if the *Liberty* had been identified in her true operational role, at worst her presence might draw some verbal political attack from the Russians or the Russian-Arab alliance. Even this would probably take the form of private protests at military attaché level in Washington.

Naval officers were paid to operate their ships and fight when and if they had to. On this basis the general consensus of wardroom opinion was to ignore the irritating surveillance of the unidentified jets and to dismiss wild speculations on the consequences of it. Such consequences if and when they arose, and if they were political, were nothing to do with Commander McGonagle and his crew. Their orders were explicit and specific and they were being followed in the best unquestioning tradition of the service.

Armstrong had quoted a line of Tennyson to Kiepfer after the discussion. It was from the poet's Crimean War commemoration

35

of the Charge of the Light Brigade of Cavalry against the Russian guns at Balaclava: 'theirs not to reason why, theirs but to do or die'. To which Kiepfer had replied 'Not on this trip', and Armstrong had gone topside grinning.

McGonagle meanwhile was considering his options in case *Liberty* met any actual interference as a result of the surveillance. He knew there was a large Russian 'fishing' fleet in the area and that the Russian 'trawlers' he had sighted the previous day had similar equipment and operational procedure to his own ship, but were backed by heavier fire power. In addition to two banks of heavy machine guns similar to his own, they would carry 80mm cannon fore and aft hidden by their false superstructure, and sometimes even two torpedo tubes mounted either side of the bow together with depth charges. He had also received an unconfirmed report that there were two Russian missile cruisers in the area in addition to the forthcoming cruiser *Moskva*. They had passed through the Bosporus Straits only two days before, each carrying missile-bearing helicopters which gave them short-strike air potential and air-to-ground missile attacking range. The cruisers and their aerial hardware were the Russians' only challenge to the carriers *Saratoga* and *America* and even that challenge was a procedural one. No real defiance was intended. The NATO Turkey Agreement allowing Russian warships from the Black Sea to the Mediterranean through the Bosporus barred any passage of aircraft carriers, allowing the USSR had them, which it did not. Russian sea-air strike power was based solely on the use of jump jets or Ka-25 Hormone B form helicopters from Kresta 1 class cruisers. These cruisers were not barred passage through the Straits, and moved freely between the Mediterranean and the Soviet Black Sea Fleet.

So the opposition ranged against the USS *Liberty* was only the unlikely threat of Soviet cruisers or one of the Echo-class missile submarines which could be anywhere. Nothing remained of the Egyptian Navy. There were Israeli patrol boats, but they were considered allies. But there was never time for complacency on a ferret. McGonagle's orders were to keep a 'low profile'. Both Egypt and Israel claimed a twelve-mile offshore territorial limit, so the first prudent measure was to take up a cruising position well outside this boundary. McGonagle continued to run *Liberty* west by south and parallel to the Gaza coastline but on a position exactly fourteen miles on a reading fixed from the minaret of the mosque at Al Arish.

He also arranged a cover story with Lieutenant-Commander Armstrong, his ship's Intelligence Officer Lieutenant Ennis and Major Allen Blue the NSA intelligence coordinator, in the event that the *Liberty* should be boarded by Israeli, Russian or Egyptian personnel. To the Russians and Egyptians they would admit a general 'watching brief' for the US Sixth Fleet which the Soviets would not like but could hardly object to, since their trawlers were engaged in identical operations themselves and the circumstances of these operations were well known to the *Liberty*. In the event of an Israeli boarding, McGonagle would state the *Liberty*'s mission as 'monitoring Soviet radar systems and Arab radio communications with the Soviet Mediterranean naval presence'.

The Captain had inquired of Major Blue if there was the slightest possibility that *Liberty*'s coded transmissions had been intercepted and decoded. This could be the reason why someone, somewhere, was keeping her under observation. Major Blue had replied that this was not merely unlikely but impossible. There had been no evidence through static blackout, transmission output or incoming reception that there was any sort of intercept or interference. *Liberty* was in direct contact with the NSA at Fort Meade through the CIA radio communications centre at Asmara, Ethiopia, and their frequency was staggered both in timing and direction to confuse any electronics surveillance of transmissions. At irregular intervals, transmissions and incoming messages were travelling through posts in Italy, Turkey and Iran, to stagger the use of Asmara.

McGonagle inquired if the radio room had received any sort of indirect contact with the watching jets. He received a negative reply. Major Blue had noted from the radar/sonar read-out from the large-impulse interception 'big ear' mounted above *Liberty*'s bridge that the size of the jets indicated they could be any type of medium-range interceptor-assault fighters. They were definitely not long-range bomber class aircraft, which meant they were not purpose-built spy planes like the US Air Force B52s or P3 Orions,

37

or a Russian Ilyushin 11-28. Also there had been no sign on the probes of any electronic gadgetry being activated, which meant that the aircraft were not electronic activity centres engaged in any sort of close liaison with seaborne craft. The final aircraft, sighted by radar showings indicating size and speed, was probably a Dakota or a Noratlas. If it was on surveillance it would almost certainly be using long-range aerial-photography equipment mounted in the nose.

Commander McGonagle seemed outwardly unconcerned. He was always quiet and contained even in crisis. It was his shell. While every command is lonely and hard, perhaps the loneliest and the hardest is the command of an intelligence unit. In the world of intelligence you are never quite sure you know everything and what little you do know you can rarely discuss with others because personal confidence is rigidly limited to suit the murky secret status of professional spying.

Because of the unusual liaison with the Polaris submarine, McGonagle's main concern, if his ship was under close surveillance, was to make sure the *Andrew Jackson* was not discovered. *Andrew Jackson* was now cruising parallel with and below *Liberty* in a condition of 'readiness stage Red One' even though the US Mediterranean Fleet had not yet been placed in battle order by the Joint Chiefs of Staff in Washington. If *Liberty* was exposed at close quarters then there was a chance *Andrew Jackson* would also be discovered. McGonagle was convinced the submarine had not yet been discovered. While Russia might complain about a US covert intelligence ship, the discovery of an armed Polaris submarine in a battle zone where America had declared an interest, if not intent, for one side, could constitute grounds for a serious confrontation which could easily escalate into open US–Soviet naval hostilities. Egypt could also justifiably make international representations on the grounds that the presence of an American nuclear sub in that area at that time, international coastal limits aside, was a positive act of aggression by the US towards Egypt. In military politics the disposition of the US submarine could and would be construed by the opposition as active US support for Israel's aggression against Egypt. At the conference with Blue, Ennis and Armstrong, McGonagle was told

38

by Major Blue that no further communication would be made between *Liberty* and the *Andrew Jackson* until the observations and sweeps *Liberty* was making precluded any interference or surveillance by outsiders, hostile or otherwise.

Conference ended at 12.45 p.m. To keep the crew alert but without suggesting it was an emergency measure, McGonagle ordered a general stand-to. This was a regular combat alert procedure carried out by all operational US naval vessels. It included the manning of the forward and after machine guns. It took place between 1.10 p.m. and 1.48 p.m.

Although McGonagle would have felt the ship more secure on a full alert, he did not wish to alarm his crew. He was also conscious of the need to keep the deck of his ship as it had been for the last few days so that there would be no show of the 'neutral' ship in a state of warlike preparation if it continued under surveillance.

The crew had seen the planes and there had been speculation about them in the fo'c's'le and on the mess deck. After the stand-to some of the older hands muttered about 'the Rooskis', but let it pass. Until the moment of actual attack, if any came, 'the Rooskis' were the problem of the brass.

McGonagle went below to the wardroom for a cold salad lunch and coffee. It was hot on deck. With only a slight breeze blowing from the north-east, the noon sun had pushed the temperature to the high eighties.

The Captain was still outwardly unconcerned but inwardly he was bothered. He had thought and rethought his position and the quality of the material his Communications Room had already passed to Fort Meade. The central monitoring work done so far had not concerned Russian radar, Russian naval movements or Arab troop movements but concentrated on the disposition of Israeli forces. The ship had been specifically asked by the NSA that morning to keep a close watch on the progress of Israeli troops along the Jordanian fronts, particularly the West Bank and the Old City of Jerusalem. There was also a request to close-monitor events on the Syrian front along the Golan Heights above the Plain of Galilee. Any Israeli pushes across the borders as established and legalized by the UN were to be reported in detail as they happened. The reports also had to include, if possible, details of Israeli aircraft and armour, their disposition and their strength.

Captain McGonagle and Major Blue had sent two requests for clarification of orders to Fort Meade. Should *Liberty* proceed, move closer and continue to monitor, or should she retreat towards the Sixth Fleet, because her mission had been exposed? Also, because Israeli victory was by now assured, the primary mission with *Andrew Jackson* could safely be aborted. However vague the surveillance was and by whatever interested party, the ship's mission had been discovered and possibly her communications had been monitored. McGonagle expected some word by return but no word came. So now he waited and, like a good officer, while he waited he carried on as ordered.

McGonagle had been in the wardroom three or four minutes when Armstrong heard the planes. He was on the bridge fixing a new course for *Liberty* and checking it against the radar. As he became aware of the planes the lookout came up. 'Aircraft in the immediate area, sir. The Chief says they are turning towards the ship, sir.'

Armstrong crossed to the starboard side of the bridge and took the aircraft in sight with his binoculars. They appeared to be of the same type he had seen early in the morning. They were coming in fast and low. Armstrong turned to Quartermaster Francis Brown, the senior non-com on the bridge. 'Take the wheel, Chief.'

'Yes, sir.'

'By God,' Armstrong said, 'these guys look as though they mean business.'

Two or three men forward of the wheelhouse waved angrily as the fighters came streaming in.

Armstrong was running for the klaxon to sound battle stations when the first battery of cannon and rockets hit the ship, shaking and rolling her like a tiny dinghy in white water. He could see three jets in triangular attack formation. They could have been MIGS but Armstrong was still thinking fast. 'Mirages!' he shouted to the quartermaster. 'My God, they're Mirages. Can't they see our flag?'

Commander McGonagle was already up the companionway which led from the wardroom. Dr Kiepfer was running for the infirmary. The men in the crew quarters were just being reassigned after general assembly and the first blast threw a group of them off their feet. One of the men, Seaman Fred Kerner of Scranton, New Jersey, was thrown against the bulkhead. Someone was shouting that the boiler had blown. McGonagle and his officers and non-coms were pouring into the afternoon sunshine. The Mirages were banking for another run. The decks were covered with bodies, some moving, some still. Men were crawling, crying, bleeding. The decking and the wheelhouse superstructure forward was ripped to shreds by cannon and machine-gun fire. A plume of black smoke was swirling from a blazing rubber liferaft.

McGonagle stared for a moment across the deck. He had dreamed of such things as he now saw, but only in nightmares. Now it was real.

The Mirages came streaking back, still in their deadly battle triangle. The Putt! Putt! Putt! rattle of the twelve wing-mounted heavy machine guns drowned out the cries of the wounded. Bullets tore into the bodies forward and aft. They cut up the dead, the dying and the frightened, hurling them about like rag dolls. The strafing fire ran the length of the ship in straight following lines. Later it could only be described in a hackneyed cliché: bullets rained on the deck like hailstones. Nothing else could describe the moments of the strafing run. Eloquence would be wasted on it. Only the cliché was good. Death swept across the ship like the dark clouds which always come with a sudden summer squall. One moment there was sunshine. The next, blackness.

The decks splintered under the impact of the heavy machine-gun bullets. Then there were more explosions and the crash of falling superstructure as *Liberty* began to give under the heavy pressure of the attack. The ship was being torn apart.

Three runs had been made by the Mirages in almost as many minutes. McGonagle was trying to reorganize his command from the bridge when he heard a seaman yelling that a single aircraft was coming in from port making an attack amidships across the beam. The seaman, Richard Weaver, dived under a bulkhead for cover closely followed by a pattern of machine-gun bullets which chewed up the deck boards and clattered against the hull with loud whining ricochets.

Weaver crouched in the foetal position, his legs drawn up to his

41

stomach, trying to make himself as small a target as possible. He thought he heard the track of bullets pass him by. Then there was a loud explosion. It seemed to be on top of him, even inside his head. He got to his feet to run to some other shelter. He felt a blow in the pit of his stomach. He staggered, fell to his knees and got up again to continue towards a companionway door. He felt hot liquid all around his groin and thought he must be sweating too much because he was so scared. He put his hand inside his pants waistband and it came out wet and sticky and covered in warm blood. Fred Kerner grabbed Weaver and pulled him inside. 'Hey there, Dick. Let's get you down to sick bay.'

Weaver leaned hard against Kerner, his eyes wide and unblinking 'I'm shot. I'm hit.'

Kerner pulled Weaver into sick bay. It was already filling up with men. Lieutenant Kiepfer had one on the operating table to tourniquet the bleeding from a burst leg artery. An orderly took Weaver. 'Put him over there with the others.'

He indicated a corner of bleeding men, some lying on the floor, others propped against the bulkhead. 'We'll deal with him when we can. How bad is he?'

'He's alive and conscious.'

'OK. Leave him there.'

Kerner went back up the companionway. The decks were strewn with dead and wounded men and wreckage. The sun was blotted out by a rising canopy of smoke. The air reeked of cordite, blazing neoprene and burnt flesh. As Kerner came out of the companionway the jets flew in again. This time they were in two pairs. McGonagle yelled to Lieutenant Toth to get outside and make a positive identification of the planes. 'They're coming in across the beam and fore to aft. If they're Israeli planes try to make a signal.'

Toth went to the forward open platform of the bridge, swinging his glasses at the jets coming in towards the bow of the *Liberty*. He probably never saw the two flashes of the rockets leaving their pods from the Mirage to port. One of the rockets hit the bridge, enveloping Toth in a mass of flame and smoke. He died instantly. McGonagle was blown off his feet by the impact of the missile. Armstrong helped him up.

The captain waved towards two 55-gallon gasoline cans, blazing on the starboard side of the ship. 'Phil, get forward and clear away those oil drums.'

Armstrong started down the companionway ladder with Lieutenant O'Connor close behind. A Mirage was coming in from starboard, firing its four wing-mounted machine guns. As it closed on the ship it released its last two rockets from their pods. One rocket hit the starboard bulkhead just ahead of the bridge. Its blast knocked both officers off their feet. Shrapnel from the detonation almost cut Armstrong in half. O'Connor was hit by some smaller shrapnel fragments but was able to regain his feet, though dazed. He turned to Armstrong and saw he was beyond help.

'O'Connor. Are you all right?'

McGonagle too had been blown off his feet by the blast and taken some cuts from flying shrapnel and glass.

'Yes, sir. Mr Armstrong's dead.'

'All right, O'Connor. Get down to sick bay and see the MO, then get back up here if you can. I need every officer who can crawl.'

'Yes, sir.'

McGonagle turned to Quartermaster Brown. 'Full ahead, all engines, Mr Brown!'

McGonagle turned to his senior radio officer, Lieutenant Maurice Bennet of Pittsburgh.

'Report to the Chief of Naval Operations we are under attack by unidentified jet aircraft. Immediate assistance required. Tell the Communications Room to pass on the message on all closed and open circuits. Inform the shadow we may have to abandon ship and will require immediate pickup. Pass the same message on to the USS *Little Rock*.'

'Yes, sir.'

'And Bennet, put out an open-channel Mayday. Put out everything, everywhere.'

'Yes, sir.'

Bennet made his way down to the radio room. He met Lieutenant Ennis in the hatchway.

'The Captain has ordered all full transmissions reporting our condition as under attack by unidentified aircraft to go to *Little*

Rock and Chief of Naval Operations. Also, he said to put out a general open-channel Mayday.'

The radio operator was already working. 'Most of the equipment is out, sir,' he told Ennis. 'The masts must have been damaged.'

The constant and accurate fire by rockets and machine guns sustained now for a full nine minutes had wrecked the antennae of the ship. The pattern of fire indicated these masts had been the initial primary target.

'The general line is still open,' the radio operator said.

'OK,' Ennis told him, 'open channel general distress.'

The operator tapped the keys. 'Mayday. Mayday. Am under attack from jet aircraft. Last position 14·26 miles north-west of Al Arish proceeding north-west approximately 12 knots. Immediate assistance required.' The message ended. The transmission light flashed off for the last time as the Mirages came back to continue their lacerating cross-fire on *Liberty*. The worst was now to come. The planes were turning, attacking, turning, attacking. In the next six minutes they made four more runs across the ship, strafing with machine guns and cannon. (A later count was to show 821 separate hits on *Liberty*'s hull and superstructure.) In addition to the cannon and machine-gun fire the jets had scored direct hits with at least six rockets and had dropped incendiaries on the forward and after decks and across the superstructure.

McGonagle decided not to man the forward and after Browning machine guns. They would have little or no effect on the Mirages and would certainly draw fire from the jets. The only chance was to run. Smoke was pouring from the damaged quarters of the ship, providing some providential shelter. McGonagle decided to add to it.

Bennet was back on the bridge.

'Mr Bennet, give us covering smoke.'

'Quartermaster Brown, keep her running west by north as parallel as possible to the coastline in case we have to abandon.'

McGonagle rang down to the Communications Room. 'How're you men doing down there?'

'OK, Captain.' It was Ennis who answered. 'Seems most of the equipment is non-operational because we've lost all of our antennae but radar is fifty per cent operational and we have our shadow showing on a course and speed level with us at a depth of 200 feet.'

'OK,' McGonagle said, 'I guess they'll stay there. Nothing they can do against aircraft anyway.'

The *Andrew Jackson*'s surface potential was little better than *Liberty*'s: one heavy 50-calibre Browning machine gun and four 21-inch conventional torpedoes. She did carry ground-to-air non-nuclear missiles but her position and situation were too delicate to allow their use. Unless *Andrew Jackson* was put under specific attack she had to have any offensive action sanctioned by the Joint Chiefs of Staff. Whether or not she had made representations to Washington via the USS *Little Rock*, McGonagle did not know. His training told him that unless it was a question of *Liberty*'s final life or death, the *Andrew Jackson* would obey orders, lie silent and maintain a watching brief. However, there was reassurance in the knowledge that the submarine was there and that she would have been alerted by the very first transmissions from *Liberty*.

The jets were coming in again but this time there were only two, running in from the bows and striking down towards the stern.

McGonagle was thinking clearly and carefully. He had seen markings on the sides of the Mirages and, despite the speed of the planes and the hampering smoke and the distractions around him, he was sure they were Israeli Air Force. If he and his ship survived the attack the identity of the assailants was sure to become a matter of dispute. The captain fished into the wheelhouse locker and brought out a small viewfinder Cannon camera loaded with Kodak Tri-X film. The Mirages were coming in on a long, low run, a rocket run. McGonagle's left arm was bleeding and too stiff to raise and flex his fingers so he worked the camera one-handed with his good right arm, his thumb levering the film transport and his forefinger squeezing the shutter. It was impossible to keep the Mirages in clear focus. In the light made murky by fumes and smoke McGonagle had to use maximum aperture at maximum speed. He shot at 1/500 of a second at F 5·6 and hoped that this would be good enough. As the jets flashed across the smoke stack he worked the camera, winding on and shooting almost continuously.

A seaman from the Communications Room now appeared at

the top of the bridge companion ladder and handed McGonagle a report from the radar room. Three boats had been picked up astern coming from a south-easterly direction but changing course slightly to the north and travelling at a speed of 30-plus knots.

McGonagle put down the camera and picked up the report, hearing the jets make a loud screaming turn astern. He was starting to read when another explosion shook the bridge, and he felt a heavy impact on his right leg followed by a searing pain. His knees started to buckle but he leaned against the bulkhead, blinking and shaking his head to stop himself fainting. He looked down at his torn trousers and saw the blood pumping from a gash that ran from his knee down to his calf. His foot was sticky warm from the blood filling his shoe.

In his later report Commander McGonagle dismissed the incident in a few lines: 'I was knocked off my feet completely. I was only shaken up and it made me dance around a little bit but my injuries did not appear to be of any consequence. I noticed slight burns on my left forearm and blood oozing on my right trouser leg. Since I could walk and there was no apparent pain I gave no further consideration to these minor injuries.' Unbelievably, as though the whole thing was a short but never-ending nightmare, it was now only 2.24 p.m. In twenty minutes of full battle conditions Commander William McGonagle had already earned himself the Congressional Medal of Honour. . .

Lieutenant Bennet who had been forward to check the damage came back up the bridge companion ladder.

'Lookouts report three MTBs approaching from the north-east. They're running in triangular formation at between 27 and 30 knots. It looks like they're coming in for a hit, Captain.'

McGonagle did not pause to consider this new adversary. His order followed the second Bennet finished: 'Tell the forward machine guns to take them under fire the moment they come into range,' he said.

The tannoy had gone when the rest of the communications equipment was destroyed by enemy fire. McGonagle shouted to a group of seamen close to the bridge: 'Pass the word along, men. Stand by for torpedo attack.'

Now the captain needed all his powers of concentration. They would come in and try to hit his ship forward, amidships and astern to achieve a fast sinking. The pattern of attack offered no quarter. McGonagle now knew for certain what he had already guessed. Whoever had ordered the attack intended to kill his ship and every man on it. Their only chance lay in the captain's ability to manoeuvre fast to avoid the first clutch of torpedoes, then try to figure out the second attack pattern and take as little damage as possible. There was no way to avoid less than two hits from a total of six torpedo launches. Each MTB would be carrying two metal fish; they would fire one each simultaneously on the first run and then strike individually on the second run if *Liberty* had not already gone by then.

The chance of avoiding total destruction on the second run would be many thousands to one. Unless McGonagle had unbelievable luck he would take one hit at least in the first attack which would certainly disable his steering gear at least in part, if not altogether.

Concentrating hard between increasingly frequent flashes of pain Commander McGonagle carefully studied his course. He decided to hold steady until the last moment and then turn hard to port, making *Liberty* a smaller target for a second attack run when it came. Moving seaward would be fatal. It would bring his ship broadside on to the attack pattern of the MTBs and make it an easier target.

'Mr Bennet,' he said, 'the jackstaff has been shot away; we are no longer showing a flag. Tell the signalman to hoist our holiday ensign from the yardarm. Show the bastards our colours again.'

The holiday ensign is a ceremonial Stars and Stripes measuring 7' X 13'. A signalman hoisted it to the yardarm. It hung limply for a moment then streamed out in *Liberty*'s wake.

The men on the almost stricken ship now watched the MTBs coming, knowing there was little they could do but pray. The boats were about a mile astern and still moving fast, maintaining triangular formation. McGonagle watched them through his binoculars. For a brief second he thought he saw a flash of a signal lamp but it could just as easily have been the sun striking the wheelhouse glass of one of the boats. He also thought he could see a blue and white flag, the Israeli Star of David, but he was not

47

absolutely certain. He said to Quartermaster Brown, 'They look like Israeli boats but I can't say for sure. Whoever they are they sure as hell know who we are and they're trying to kill us all!'

Still, there might be just a chance to hold them back for a few minutes, slow them by signalling to them. The Captain knew that at least a part of his general distress signal must have been received by the Sixth Fleet; or, even if not, the *Andrew Jackson* must be monitoring the attack and would have put out its own alarm unless it was still observing total radio silence for security reasons. Almost half an hour had passed since the first airstrike. If the Sixth Fleet had ordered a scramble from the *Saratoga* and the *America*, it would take thirty to forty minutes at most for a squadron of Skyhawks, Intruders or Corsairs to cover the 600 miles to reach *Liberty*'s approximate position and then pick up the ship's exact location by fixed sighting.

Liberty's starboard signal light had been knocked out during the airstrike, so McGonagle now had Bennet try to make an identification signal with a hand-held Aldis lamp. Bennet worked the lamp, flashing *Liberty*'s recognition code. The MTBs did not slow or pause. They kept coming.

'Very well, Mr Bennet, leave the Aldis, order the forward starboard gun to take the boats under fire.'

Bennet yelled through the smoke and the Browning coughed out three long bursts. Sharp puffs of smoke from the MTBs, followed by a series of sharp explosions around the forward machine guns, indicated return cannon fire. The Browning stopped firing; the gunner was dead.

For a moment there was silence then the after machine gun opened up.

'Tell that gunner to hold his fire until he's received the order,' McGonagle shouted.

Someone on the deck shouted back, 'He's dead, Skipper. The goddam machine gun is shootin' off all by itself.'

The crew on the deck watched the Browning spitting out a continuous fire towards the MTBs. Heat had ignited its magazine belt and the gun, jammed on automatic fire, was taking the belt through its breach and pumping the 50-calibre shells at the MTBs.It was a remarkable, eerie sight. The firing only stopped when the belt was empty.

The MTBs were now close enough to pour machine-gun fire at the *Liberty* and knock out any further resistance from her deck guns. They were no more than 800 to 1000 yards away and there was now no doubt about their identity. The Israeli flag was plainly visible. Heavy fire poured into *Liberty*, one of the first bursts killing the helmsman, Quartermaster Brown.

McGonagle had to take the wheel himself. His eyes never left the sea around the MTBs and he now saw the first white line of a torpedo running in towards the stern of the ship. He rang down for more speed. *Liberty* kicked a little harder. The torpedo passed the stern by no more than twenty-five yards. The captain then swung hard to port, anticipating a metal fish forward. He did not see it but was sure it had missed. There was now only number three and he could see no sign of it.

Two minutes later, at 2.35 p.m. exactly, the ship was hit on the starboard side immediately forward of the bridge and a few feet below the waterline. *Liberty* shuddered under the impact of the explosion which blew a hole in her side that extended from just above the waterline to below the turn of the bilges.

The hole was shaped like a teardrop and measured 39 feet across at its widest point. It was dead centre of the Communications Room, and ripped it apart, destroying most of the equipment and killing twenty-five men, including the CIA Major, Allen Blue.

Liberty immediately took a nine-degree list to starboard. Power and steering were lost just as the captain had feared they would be. She came to a dead halt, stopped, swung with the tide and hove to, crippled in the oily sea. There was no way the captain could manoeuvre to avoid the death blow. It was 2.36 p.m.

The planes should be here, the Captain thought. Why the hell aren't they here? Where are they? Did our messages get through? What's the *Jackson* doing? Are they going to let these bastards finish us off?

McGonagle took the MTBs into view with his glasses. For some reason they had stopped about half a mile astern of *Liberty*. Why were they not making a killing run on the *Liberty*? Perhaps they were just going to fire their torpedoes at the ship without approaching any closer. After all, *Liberty* was in range. She was a true sitting duck.

49

The captain peered through the smoke at the enemy boats. He thought he saw a light. Then he was sure he did. He watched the blink, blink of the signal lamp and scribbled quickly on the bridge receiving pad. The signal read 'Do you need assistance?'

Not sure that the MTBs would read a weak signal from an Aldis, McGonagle ordered a signalman to hoist the international sign 'Not under control'. Delaying tactics of any kind was the captain's only hope.

The MTBs made no answer; they just continued to drift silently along in the current, standing off from the crippled American ship.

McGonagle watched them for a while and after fifteen minutes he began to feel almost sure that for some reason they now did not intend to kill him and his ship, but why he did not know.

Lieutenant Kiepfer came up to the bridge and advised the captain to go below for treatment.

'What's it like down there, Doctor?'

'Like a charnel house.'

'Then you don't need me. Give me a pain killer.'

'You need treatment, sir.'

'So do the others. More than me. I'm still walking and thinking at least. Anyway, my deck officers are all either dead or wounded. I'll stay on up here, Doctor, until we're either safe or we're all dead.'

When the captain turned back to watch his enemies again they had gone. The horizon was empty. He could not even see the wakes of the departing boats. Then the captain saw the conn-trails high in the blue sky of two formations of banking jets. He could not see who they were, but he could guess: they were the planes of the US Navy, sent out in response to *Liberty*'s radioed calls for help.

As the conn-trails banked east and then north-west towards the horizon which hid their base carriers *Saratoga* and *America*, and the land base at Suda Bay, Crete, where the heavy Skyhawk fighter-bombers had to land, two jets swung in from the south-east, approached the ship and circled it several times.

McGonagle limped onto the forward bridge and watched these planes make three more circuits of the ship and then level off in the direction from which they had appeared. The captain identified both planes through his field glasses as Israeli Mirage tactical fighters, probably two of the same planes that had attacked his ship. But he was sure now that *Liberty* and her remaining crew were safe. However, he was unable to even imagine what turn the drama would next take. He supposed the MTBs had returned to base. Since they had each fired only one torpedo he was sure they had not left to rearm and recommence their assault. McGonagle had considered they might launch a night assault to put a boarding party on his ship and secure his communications equipment. As an extreme safety measure he would have considered destroying every piece of classified material aboard, but the Israeli torpedo boats had already done that.

He was certain that the biggest group of conn-trails were American aircraft and that the Israelis had withdrawn before they became vulnerable to attack by the US fighters. The crippled ship had been left to sink or to survive as best she could. Having survived this far, the captain determined he was not going to sink.

He looked hard at the bullet- and shell-riddled hulk of his ship and then turned to Lieutenant Bennet: 'Damage reports from all quarters. Have the Chief Engineer report to me on the double.'

'Yes, sir.'

The Chief Engineer was on the bridge moments later.

'Tell me, Chief, how are those engines shaping up?'

'OK, Captain. We should have power pretty soon. A damage detail is patching up the holes. The torpedo damage will obviously slow us down a lot but providing we don't meet any storms we should be able to keep up power in this calm sea to get us at least as far as the Fleet.'

He had barely finished when the engines juddered for a moment then burst into life.

'There go the engines, Captain. Now we only need to get the steering gear fixed, and I don't know how long that will take or even if it can be done. It took a battering.'

'Don't even try then, Chief. Have a detail go down to the after steering compartment and get a field telephone line rigged between there and the bridge. I will conn and helm the ship myself. I'll call the orders over the phone and have the ship ruddered by hand. The details can work down there four hours on in shifts.'

51

'Yes, sir.'

'All right then, Chief, we'll get under way. Mr Bennet!'

'Yes, sir?'

'We are going to steam ahead with a detail working the hand rudder in the after steering compartment. Place the ship on full alert, check, rearm and man the forward and after machine guns and double the lookouts.'

'Yes, sir.'

Soon an engineer came onto the bridge to report the telephone rigged and working and the detail in the after steering compartment awaiting orders.

The captain picked up the telephone. He ordered a course set west by north, rang down 'ahead' and the *Liberty* began to limp slowly towards the now sinking sun.

She had been moving for barely forty minutes when at 4.15 p.m. a helicopter appeared from the south-east. Lieutenant Bennet came up to the bridge.

'Helicopter reported from a south-easterly direction, sir. It appears to be carrying Israeli markings but there are no signs of any exposed armaments.'

'Right, Mr Bennet. Order the machine gunners to take it in sight but to hold fire until I tell them otherwise. That chopper is coming too slow and straight to be on an attack pattern. I believe they just want to have a good look at us.'

The helicopter flew over *Liberty*, circled and then dropped down to a height of about fifty feet above the ship's stack. Someone leaned out through the open door and shouted to the ship through a megaphone.

McGonagle was unable to hear for the first few moments, then he picked out the words in English. 'We have medical orderlies on board. What are your injuries?'

The captain limped onto the forward bridge and made a derisory gesture aimed straight at the helicopter. 'Go to hell!' he yelled through his own megaphone.

The helicopter voice shouted again; a ladder was lowered and a man started to climb down.

'I told you to go to hell. You're not coming on my ship. Go to hell, you bastards.' Still speaking through the megaphone

52

McGonagle shouted to the forward gunner. 'Take the helicopter under sight. If they make any move to board this ship you will open fire on them without further orders.'

'Understood, sir.'

The man on the ladder hurried back into the helicopter. A signal light flashed ordering McGonagle to stop. He ignored it. The helicopter then swung to the stern of the *Liberty*, came in low and dropped something onto the deck. It was a weight with a card sellotaped to it. It was the calling card of Commander Ernest Castle, naval attaché to the American Embassy in Tel Aviv. On the back of the card was scrawled almost illegibly in biro 'Have you any casualties?'

McGonagle read this most cryptic query. He was going to pick up the megaphone to reply, but was too overwhelmed by the stupidity of it to think of anything adequate in reply. Instead he pointed, first at the helicopter, then at three bodies lying on the deck in pools of blood and at the men still carrying their wounded comrades to the sick bay. He gestured for the helicopter to leave. He rang to the engine room: 'Keep going, Chief. We have company topside but they are not stopping us now.'

'OK, sir.'

Liberty continued on her course. The helicopter stayed with her, but only after retiring to a height of about 500 feet.

The sun was setting into a blue-red sky which pleased McGonagle because it indicated settled weather. The wind was steady and light, north-easterly. The sky promised another clear, calm day to follow. As the sun finally set just after 7 p.m., the helicopter turned back towards the land. McGonagle now knew it was over for sure. He and his little ship had won when all the odds said they were finished.

Chapter Five

The captain was pleased when darkness came less than thirty minutes after the helicopter had disappeared. There was something secure in the blanket of it even though there was a bright moon and a clear sky full of stars. It would be a beautiful night to make a sail boat trip, the captain thought. He thought about the many weekends he had spent in sailing boats running up the coast from Norfolk, Virginia, sometimes as far as Chintogue or down the Carolina coast off Hiltonhead.

He watched his course on the compass and called each correction down the telephone line to the after steering compartment. After an hour Lieutenant Kiepfer came on to the bridge and asked the captain to go below to sick bay for treatment. McGonagle refused.

'Mr Kiepfer,' he said. 'I have no intention of leaving this bridge or the command of my ship until we have at least made contact with the Fleet. I only require something to help keep me awake and alert.'

'Very good, sir.'

Ten years later Lieutenant-Commander Kiepfer would sit in his office at the US Navy Nuclear Research Laboratory at Bethesda, Maryland, and repeat exactly what he told a court of inquiry about his captain's attitude.

'The commanding officer was like a rock upon which the men supported themselves. To know that he was grievously wounded and yet having to conn and helm the ship through the night, calling every change of course, was the thing that told the men "we're going to live". When I went to the bridge and saw this I should say that I knew I could only insult this man by insisting that he be taken below for treatment to his wounds.'

Kiepfer made very little of his own role, despite the Silver Star he was awarded for it, refusing to admit that without the dedicated struggle he and his corpsmen made to keep the sick bay working

54

efficiently and effectively, the final casualty figure would have shown at least one-third dead more than was actually the case.

The doctor and his men worked continuously for twenty-eight hours in overcrowded conditions and so desperately short of drugs that they had to ration them to all but the most desperately wounded. During the actual battle, Kiepfer had been able to do little more than administer first aid. But the high degree of his dedication and care helped save the life of many seriously wounded sailors. McGonagle had saved the ship but it was Kiepfer who had saved the crew. Through his twenty-eight hours at the operating tables and stretchers of the sick bay, he administered morphine, treated for shock, drained blood from flooded lungs and carried out one transfusion after another so that in the end he could not even begin to remember the final tally of his efforts.

Dr Kiepfer was not a field surgeon, but circumstances forced him to undertake actions that tested his skills to their limits. Being the only qualified man present, he did not hesitate, thus following the best traditions of his profession.

The men in the sick bay helped him. In the most desperate moments, listening to the noise of battle outside and expecting at any moment a bomb, a rocket or a torpedo to rip them apart, they were inspired by the courage of their doctor to work alongside him if they could. Whenever Kiepfer needed a volunteer to give blood he would get ten. Whatever he asked for, the men volunteered, even the bedridden and the crippled.

'There has been a lot written and said about the Navy, but no ship in any action, even in World War II, had more courage than that little *Liberty*,' Kiepfer said. 'The courage wasn't just in the captain or in the crew but in the ship. Everyone felt for the ship and when she was limping home we were all reassured by her. We loved that little ship. We knew the captain had saved us but we felt the ship had saved us too by refusing to sink. So did the captain. Somehow I felt he really did not want to go home. He just wanted to stay there with *Liberty*, even though she was shot to hell. They never broke the spirit of that little ship. They punished her and crippled her but she got right back up and limped away from them. They couldn't beat her down.'

On the bridge, Commander McGonagle was beginning to feel

faint and periodically he would drag himself to his feet, limp outside onto the forward front and suck in great gulps of the fresh breeze to clear his head.

Shortly after midnight he decided to stay outside in the fresh air and lay on the deck of the bridge wing with his injured leg propped high against the bulkhead to stop the bleeding. Although becoming delirious, he retained command, refusing to relax completely or hand over his control to any other man.

As McGonagle lay on the bridge wing, half-thinking and half-dreaming, but alert and determined, knowing he had won the day, it seemed incredible when he actually allowed himself to think about it, that his ship had been attacked, had fought back, had recovered and was returning home, all in less than twelve hours. Since there was now time to think against the steady drum of *Liberty*'s engines and the hiss of her propeller wake, the Captain allowed himself to consider speculatively what had gone on in other places, how other people had reacted: the captain of the *Andrew Jackson*, his superiors, his Fleet Admiral, the Generals at the NSA and the Joint Chiefs of Staff, the Director of the CIA, the President.

The engineers were restoring adequate communication links so he would soon be able to talk to the Sixth Fleet but he wondered just what had happened to the *Jackson*. Had she remained on station? Was she shadowing *Liberty* until the latter contacted the Sixth Fleet, which must now be steaming forward to intercept her? Was *Liberty* still being shadowed by the Israelis? What were they saying in Washington? If the Naval Attaché in Tel Aviv was involved in this thing, there must be a terrible stink along the communication lines from Washington to Tel Aviv.

McGonagle decided he did not really care why the Israelis had decided to attack his ship. He was only interested in consequences. From the count given by Lieutenant Bennet and Dr Kiepfer he had 28 dead (the final total would be 34) and 171 wounded including himself. Out of his crew of 279 this represented a casualty total of over seventy per cent.

Perhaps it would have cheered him to know that his penultimate superiors, the Joint Chiefs of Staff in Washington, had met in hastily convened emergency session just after 9 a.m. Eastern

Standard Time that same day of the attack, and had responded to the information that *Liberty* had been raided by IDF planes and MTBs by ordering an airstrike on the Israeli naval base at Haifa. The order had been immediately countermanded by the President; but the very fact that it had been issued would have encouraged Commander McGonagle if he had known about it.

The alarm was raised when President Johnson was awakened at 7.30 a.m. by a message from his security adviser, Walt Rostow. It read: 'We have a flash report from the Joint Reconnaissance Centre indicating a US electronic intelligence ship, the *Liberty*, has been torpedoed in the Mediterranean. It is 60–100 miles north of Egypt. Reconnaissance aircraft are out from the Sixth Fleet. There is no knowledge of the submarine or surface vessel who committed this act.'

A hastily convened conference of the President's staff including Secretary of State, Dean Rusk, was told by NSA chiefs that there was still no word identifying the attackers. While the radical hawks inside and outside the White House were working themselves into a state to demand retaliatory measures against the culprits who just had to be the Reds, the tacticians at the NSA had to counsel patience, explaining there were no grounds for planning any sort of US action until more was known. They claimed to be as mystified by the circumstances of the attack as everyone else. This was a lie.

They were handing out this counsel while dealing confidentially with a detailed report coupled with an apology by the Israeli Government for the attack by their planes and torpedo boats on the *Liberty* 'by mistake'. It was only hurriedly passed to Walt Rostow in the Situation Room at the White House when the JCS on their own initiative issued orders for the airstrike by two wings of Sixth Fleet Skyhawks from the *Saratoga* and *America* on the torpedo-boat base at Haifa. Rostow gave the report to President Johnson with the advice to countermand the order immediately. Johnson's countermanding signal went to the USS *Little Rock* within minutes.

The effect of the news of an Israeli attack on the *Liberty* in the White House Situation Room was in total contrast to the way the same report had fallen on the Joint Chiefs. Where the generals had fumed at what they called 'a deliberate premeditated act of war',

57

the President and his staff reacted with almost a sigh of relief. The spectre of a Russian attack was looming so ominously at the moment when the Israeli message came, that any alternative was welcome. The implication of what the IDF had done, on the orders of the Israeli War Cabinet, was completely lost amid Johnson's anxiety over confrontation with Russia. Israel had provided him with a way out from a decision he had not wanted and did not know how to deal with. He had also been told by Rostow that if the US gave the Russians any excuse to interfere in the Middle East, that in turn would facilitate active Soviet interference in Vietnam.

At the Pentagon the JCS were outraged. Even the calm professionals at the State Department had been shaken when they inquired what immediate action was being taken and were told 'None'. A statement was issued to the press saying that Israel had attacked *Liberty* in error, that she had apologized to the United States Government and both the explanation and apology had been accepted.

That was the State Department's view. The military view was different. If the Navy could not take its retaliatory revenge then it was going to take procedural measures publicly to lay the blame for the dead and wounded and the damage to *Liberty* exactly where it belonged. A message from the Joint Chiefs to the military legation at the US Embassy in Tel Aviv ordered an immediate approach to the Government of Israel demanding a full and open inquiry into the incident. They were told such an inquiry could not be convened immediately because Israel was engaged in fighting a war.

But the Israelis had produced a token gesture for the press. Reporters in Tel Aviv were allowed to interview Micha Limor, a reservist sailor and a journalist himself who graphically described how his boat had attacked a ship 'with high masts and weird anten-nae', and how they were sure it was the 'enemy' until in the very last moments of the engagement a rubber liferaft with 'US Navy' lettering on its side had floated close to the torpedo boats 'Then,' he went on, 'helicopters came over and signalled to the torpedo boats "they are raising the American flag".'

'It was crystal clear that we had hit friends,' Limor said. He then went on to describe how his boat had tried to approach the *Liberty* to offer assistance and how an officer had appeared on the bridge for the first time and shouted 'Go to hell!' 'Realizing they would not accept aid, we left,' Limor said blandly.

To support this explanation of mistaken identity, the IDF spokesmen at the press conference told reporters that *Liberty* had been mistaken for an Egyptian supply ship, an old freighter called *El Quseir* which he claimed bore 'a remarkable superficial resemblance in shape and size to the American ship'.

Commander McGonagle and the *Liberty* were far away and too weary to care about excuses, diplomatic arguments and procedures. They had survived a murderous attack which experience told them they could not and should not have survived, and they were going home.

On the morning of 9 June they were picked up by the destroyer USS *Jefferson Davies* and tugs from the Sixth Fleet. The dead, the wounded and the survivors transferred from *Liberty* to the *Jefferson Davies* to eat and sleep and recover from the trauma of their ordeal. Commander McGonagle was treated for his wounds and slept for nearly twenty-four hours. Dr Kiepfer washed, ate his first decent hot meal in two days and collapsed into bed. 'That sleep was the best I ever had, before or since. I slept the clock round. God, I was tired!'

On 14 June, escorted by the *Jefferson Davies* and assisted by a tug, *Liberty* sailed into Valetta Harbour, Malta, with Commander McGonagle on her bridge and those of her crewmen still able to do so manning their stations.

The bullet-riddled, shell-torn ship was tied up to the quay and her captain pointed to the holes of cannon shells and rockets in her superstructure for Navy cameramen. McGonagle was proud of his ship, what she had done, and how she had survived. He was stoical and cheerful when he left *Liberty*, they all were, not knowing that she had sailed her last mission. The damage to hull and internal and external communications equipment was too severe for her to be salvaged. The 821 separate hits on the hull and superstructure alone made the *Liberty* no better than a battle hulk. War was over for the crew, too. This had been their final mission. On return to the United States they would be dispersed through other units, never to serve together again. Their captain had served his last active sea duty. Their doctor saw no more combat or the infirmary of any other ship.

Commander McGonagle was required to give evidence before a Navy Court of Inquiry at Valetta while the details of the attack were still fresh in his mind.

The Inquiry was chaired by Admiral Isaac Kidd. The Admiral was Jewish and was a strong supporter of the principles of the Israeli State. He listened carefully to Commander McGonagle's studied account of the attack which the captain of the *Liberty* presented without any attempt to introduce into it any emotion or any of his own speculation as to why it had occurred. He gave his evidence under tight self-control in the wardroom of the *Liberty* which was still pockmarked by Israeli bullets. With Admiral Kidd were Captains Bernard J. Lauff and Bert M. Atkinson, officers from the headquarters of the Commander in Chief, US Naval Forces in Europe. The atmosphere at the Inquiry was warmly and admiringly sympathetic to Commander McGonagle, who was told by Admiral Kidd that whatever politicians in Washington might want the Navy to say and whatever weak excuses the Israeli Government tried to hand out to cover its actions, they all knew that the mistaken-identity explanation was 'a goddam sneaky lie' and however watered down the findings of the inquiry would be, the Navy would insist that it went on public record as showing its scepticism to the Israeli claim.

When the findings were released publicly, a statement signed by Admiral Kidd said: 'From the time of the first attack onwards attacks were well coordinated, accurate and determined. Criss-crossing rocket and machine-gun runs from both bows, both beams and quarters effectively chewed up the entire topside including ship control and internal communications-sound powered network. Well directed initial air attack wiped out the ability of the four 50-calibre machine guns to be effective. The United States Navy wished to go on record as stating that while it had to accept the apologies of the Israeli Government it did not accept the explanation for the attack.'

He also said that as far as he was concerned the inquiry was not so much to find out what had gone wrong – they all knew about that anyway – but to record how it had all gone right and how

McGonagle and his men had pulled themselves with courage and determination in the greatest tradition of the US Navy from the proverbial jaws of death. The *Liberty*'s survival was nothing short of a miracle. Unfortunately, outside the Navy it did not matter. Heroes did not matter. Bravery had not changed the course of events. Whatever Kidd or Admiral John McCain or McGonagle or the Joint Chiefs of Staff in Washington or every surviving member of the crew of the *Liberty* thought – and they all knew damn well they had been attacked in cold blood – they had to accept they had lost the game. Because of political expediency and a frightened presidential administration in Washington, its eye on the next election and the powerful pro-Democratic Jewish vote, absolutely nothing would be done to repair the damaged honour of the US Navy and the personal hardship the killing of 34 American sailors and the maiming of another 171 had brought to so many innocent families.

Admiral Kidd's released statement was the severest censure the American Government publicly allowed, and only then under the greatest pressure from the Joint Chiefs of Staff at the Pentagon, the men President Johnson needed to fight his war in South-East Asia.

The CIA did not like it. Its Director, Richard Helms, could see that a public exposure of the Agency's Middle Eastern dirty policies would almost certainly end with heads rolling, his own first.

But there were other factors beyond the control of the American Administration and the CIA. The British Government, in their joint role with the United States as concerned supporters and de facto allies of Israel, were continuing with their own inquiries into the background and implications of the Six Day War which included, if only peripherally, an investigation into the *Liberty* incident. No help was forthcoming from the Langley headquarters of the CIA, but US Naval Intelligence within NATO was only too glad to oblige and help compile a report which had resulted from the work of Captain McKenna and other British intelligence officers operating within the war zones.

At 8 p.m. on 8 June Captain Steven McKenna had received a call from Clarkson asking him to present himself at the British Embassy immediately.

McKenna found his superior in his office with two other

61

embassy officials, one of them a military attaché and the other a Foreign Office political officer.

Clarkson asked him if he had heard about an attack by the Israelis against a ship off Gaza. McKenna said yes, he had heard the story. It was confusing. There was a suggestion that the ship was a US Navy vessel and it had been hit in mistake for an Egyptian supply ship.

The last part of the story was correct, Clarkson said. But there was some dispute about the mistake explanation. The Americans had made a formal request to British Intelligence for any assistance they could provide in dealing with the case. Clarkson wanted McKenna to accompany him to the US Embassy to meet with the Naval Attaché, Commander Ernest Castle.

At 10 a.m. the following morning Clarkson and McKenna were ushered in to see Castle. They were told by him that the attacked ship was the USS *Liberty*, a naval communications vessel temporarily attached to the Mediterranean Sixth Fleet, but working on detached duty for the National Security Agency. She had been strafed and torpedoed by the Israeli Defence Force, had sustained heavy casualties and extensive damage but was still afloat and was now limping to the NATO base at Valetta, Malta. The Israelis had apologized for the attack, saying they had mistaken the *Liberty* for an Egyptian supply ship. Commander Castle said his Government was reviewing the explanation and the apology but so far had not commented on it. The Naval Attaché added that his superiors and the National Security Agency believed the attack had been deliberate to prevent *Liberty* transmitting information to Washington which might have been used by the American Government to halt the forward movement of the Israeli Army and so prevent them from capturing territory that they had openly admitted they needed to occupy for defence reasons.

McKenna and Clarkson left the meeting with Castle and returned to the British Embassy to inform London that McKenna was returning to Cyprus and would be contactable that night at the Ledra Palace Hotel, Nicosia.

The following day, despite a demand by the United Nations for Israel to cease hostilities and respond to a declared ceasefire, the IDF attacked Syrian positions on the Golan Heights and established a forward defence perimeter inside Syrian territory.

On 14 June, McKenna was ordered to travel from the Royal Air Force base at Akrotiri, Cyprus, to Valetta. His brief contained information that a US Polaris submarine, the USS *Andrew Jackson*, had just put into Rota and a Lieutenant-Commander had been dispatched to Washington in a special US Air Force transport carrying a canister of film, which was believed to relate to the attack on the *Liberty* by the Israelis. McKenna's request to proceed immediately to Malta also contained an order to liaise with the Royal Navy base commander at Valetta and secure introductions to the US base commander and 'appreciate the situation'.

Liberty had been berthed at No. 6 Dock at Valetta. Captain McKenna walked along the quayside, studying the structural damage. He paused halfway along the ship's length and examined a torpedo hole half above and half below the waterline.

Accompanied by his guide, a US Navy Lieutenant-Commander attached to Sixth Fleet sector intelligence, he walked around the deck and bridge area where the engineer crews were working with electric arc welders to replate the holes gouged in the ship by cannon, rocket and heavy machine-gun fire. McKenna noticed the greatest concentration of hits was around the bridge and forward section of the superstructure which had obviously supported the ship's antennae. It was unnecessary to examine the ship in detail to realize that fire had been directed purposely against this area with the express intention of destroying all communication ability.

McKenna remarked on this to his American companion. The officer replied with a short and obscene remark which was, McKenna thought, a very adequate expression of the American Navy's anger and frustration over the attack. He included in his filed report to London a comment that the attitude of the US Navy and probably of the US High Command generally was 'angry and hostile' to Israel. But there had been a total and effective clampdown on all information concerning the circumstances which led to the attack and even the circumstances of the attack itself were still 'pending inquiry'.

The crew had been hurried back to the United States except for the captain and certain of his surviving officers who were to testify at a Court of Inquiry which had been convened by Admiral John

S. McCain, Commander in Chief, US Naval Forces in Europe. The Inquiry had started on 11 June and was still proceeding. (It ended on 17 June and McCain approved the findings on 18 June.)

McKenna had been given access to some of the evidence and he commented in his report that the most unusual aspect of the attack had not been the strike itself but the loss of three messages transmitted from the NSA in Washington to the *Liberty*, warning the ship that the Israelis had broken into the code bank and were monitoring American transmissions. *Liberty* was advised to abandon station's immediately and retire north-west to join the Sixth Fleet.

The alarm had been raised an hour before the first Israeli air surveillance. US Navy intelligence reported to the Joint Chiefs of Staff that Israeli monitors had broken into the *Liberty*'s coding bank, had deciphered her codes and transmitted a warning to the headquarters of Modeyin, Israel's military intelligence organization.

A message was immediately forwarded to *Liberty* by the Joint Chiefs, warning her to withdraw to the Sixth Fleet 'at once'. The message was rated by naval intelligence as 'pinnacle' which meant it had highest priority. It was to be sent through a CIA receiving and transmitting station in Asmara, Ethiopia. The message should have reached *Liberty* at 9 a.m., Middle Eastern time, but it never did. Somehow it was misrouted via Subic Bay in the Philippines and ended up, hours later, back at the NSA at Fort Meade where it was filed away in a desk drawer.

Within two hours a second message was dispatched when no response was received from *Liberty* to the first message. This one was sent to the Sixth Fleet Commander aboard the USS *Little Rock* advising of *Liberty*'s dangerous position and asking *Little Rock* in turn to advise Commander McGonagle to withdraw his ship. The *Little Rock* transmitted this advice at 11.17 a.m., again through Asmara. This message too was misrouted almost unbelievably to Port Lyautey, Morocco, and was then returned to Fort Meade and filed. The third and final message lost in the strange tangle of misroutings left the *Liberty* for the *Little Rock* via *Liberty*'s receiving station in Naples at 2.10 p.m., only seconds before *Liberty*'s communications were knocked out by the Israeli Mirages. It finally arrived at Fort Meade with the others, twelve hours later, misrouted again via Subic.

McKenna concluded that either the American system of passing pinnacle messages was so chaotic that it was totally useless which in his experience was not at all true, or else the three messages had been deliberately tampered with to delay the *Liberty* in a vulnerable position and allow the attack on the ship to be launched.

He did not speculate why this should have happened. His orders were to 'appreciate'. Occasionally in his appreciations he reached personal conclusions, which were that Israeli intelligence infiltration into the American intelligence system was so severe that they were able to follow and manipulate American secret strategy at their will and convenience. But this was only his own view. In his reports he never speculated.

However much the Johnson administration wanted to cover up the *Liberty* incident it was unable to do so totally in the face of opposition from the Pentagon and fury from the Navy Department.

On 10 June, two days after the attack, Under Secretary of State Eugene Rostow handed a note to the Israeli Ambassador in Washington, Avraham Harman, declaring the *Liberty* attack to be 'quite incomprehensible, an act of military recklessness reflecting wanton disregard for human life'. Harman sent back a reply two days later in which he rejected these charges; but diplomats in Washington and Tel Aviv continued to tell the Israelis they as yet had received 'no satisfactory explanation' for the attack. The Pentagon issued a note to the President which said, 'We cannot accept this attack as plausible under any circumstances whatsoever.'

However, in public, the matter was reviewed on the face of Israel's explanation and no one seemed able to challenge an Israeli claim that the *Liberty* had failed to identify herself just before the initial airstrike against her and had not been flying the American flag during the torpedo attack.

The Navy's frustration over the incident reached peak on 18 June when a telegram classified as confidential came into the State Department.

The subject was the Israeli Court of Inquiry into the *Liberty* attack and it was composed mainly of the points raised in a meeting between the US Naval Attaché in Tel Aviv, Commander

Castle, and a Lieutenant-Colonel Efrat, Personal Aide to General Yitzak Rabin, the Commander-in-Chief of the Israeli Defence Forces.

The telegram began with an expression of personal regret to the Commanding Officer US Navy by General Rabin for the 'sad mistake of the USS *Liberty* incident'.

It went on to say that General Rabin had decided to provide Commander Castle for his superiors with a synopsis of the findings of the IDF Court of Inquiry. This synopsis read as follows:

It is concluded, clearly and unimpeachably, from the evidence and from comparison of War Diaries that the attack on USS *Liberty* was not in malice. There was no criminal negligence and the attack was made by innocent mistake.

The attack rose out of a chain of three mistakes, each of which by itself is understandable. The first mistake was decisive. Navy and Air Force Headquarters had received a number of wrong reports stating Al Arish was being shelled from the sea. This wrong information formed the background and main factor leading to the attack on *Liberty*. The IDF Commanding Naval Officer and assistants were convinced that shelling was being done by an unidentified ship or ships which were discovered at the time near the shore of Al Arish. Even the officers who knew of the identification of *Liberty* early the same morning, did not connect *Liberty* with the unidentified ships said to be shelling Al Arish. The IDF Navy is not responsible for the mistaken report of shelling and the reasons for the mistaken report are outside the scope of the inquiry at hand. The Navy and Air Force Headquarters took the reports at full value.

The second mistake which when added to first resulted in aircraft attack on *Liberty* was a mistaken report that *Liberty* was steaming at 30 knots. This mistake had two significances: (A) When *Liberty* was identified in the morning her maximum speed was determined from Jane's Fighting Ships to be 18 knots. Therefore, even if the unidentified ship were thought to' be *Liberty* the fact that she was reported to be making 30 knots would have denied the identification.

(B) In accordance with IDF Navy Standing Orders an enemy ship in any waters which is attacking Israeli ships or shelling the Israeli shore may be attacked. If there is information of enemy ships in the area any ship or ships discovered by radar which are determined to be cruising at a speed above 20 knots may be considered an enemy. Since the speed of the unidentified ship was fixed at 28 to 30 knots, the IDF Navy was entitled to attack without further identification in view of the background of information on the shelling of Al Arish. Israeli Defence Force naval operations section had ordered the MTBs who reported *Liberty*'s speed at 30 knots to recheck and only after confirmation of that speed was the information considered reliable and aircraft were sent to attack. The question of possible negligence in establishing the speed at 28 to 30 knots, when in fact the *Liberty*'s maximum speed is 18 knots, is discounted by the IDF commanding naval officer who testified 'that such estimations require expertise and in an MTB there may be great discrepancies in fixing the speed of a vessel moving in front of it, especially if the estimate was made only over a short interval of time. It is quite feasible that there may be such a mistake, even if you measure it twice or more.' As a result of the incident maybe the Standing Order should be reconsidered but no criminal negligence is found in the MTBs' fixing of *Liberty*'s speed.

Third mistake caused execution of the second stage of attack on *Liberty* this time with torpedoes from MTBs. This was the mistaken identification of *Liberty* as the Egyptian supply ship *El Quseir*. Here I [that is, the officer conducting the inquiry who Lieutenant-Colonel Efrat identified parenthetically as Colonel Ram Ron, former Israeli Military Attaché to Washington, D.C.] must state my doubts whether the identification was not done with a certain over-eagerness as this happened when serious doubts were already beginning to arise as to the identification, as an Egyptian ship. It has been established by the Commanding Officer of the MTB division that the doubts which had begun to arise in the pilots as to their accuracy of identification did not get to the Commanding Officer of the MTB division at that time but he already knew that the ship was not a destroyer but a supply or merchant ship and this should have caused extra carefulness in identification. On the other hand, I must state the extenuating circumstances and difficulties of identification under the following conditions:

1. The ship was covered with thick smoke.
2. When asked to identify itself the ship did not do so and behaved suspiciously.
3. It appeared to the division's commander that there was a gun on the forecastle of the ship and that the ship was firing towards the MTBs. These observations were recorded in the War Diary at the time of action.

If we add to these factors that under the circumstances when the ship was completely covered with smoke there was in fact apparently a great similarity between it and *El Quseir*. Two officers, a commander and a lieutenant on two different MTBs who had no communications between them, both identified the ship at the same time as *El Quseir*. The IDF Commanding Naval Officer decided that, on the basis of the reports on hand, this identification was feasible. Therefore I have come to the conclusion that there was certainly no criminal or serious negligence in this case. Finally, I have to add that a grave additional mistake no less decisive than the three above mistakes made by the IDF was made by the *Liberty* itself. On this question I have the evidence of the IDF's Commanding Naval Officer and the Judge Advocate General which complement each other and from which it is clear that the American ship acted with lack of care by endangering itself to a grave extent by approaching excessively close to the shore in an area which was a scene of war and this at a time when it was well known that this area is not one where ships generally pass. This without advising the Israeli authorities of its presence and without identifying itself elaborately. Furthermore it appears that the ship made an effort to hide its identity first by flying a small flag which was difficult to identify from a distance; secondly, by beginning to escape when discovered by our forces and when it was aware of the fact that it had been discovered; thirdly, by failing to identify itself by its own initiative by flashing light and by refusing to do so even when asked by the MTBs. From all this I conclude that the ship *Liberty* tried to hide its presence in the area and its identity before it was discovered and even after having been attacked by the Air Force and later by the Navy and thus contributed a decisive contribution towards its identification as an enemy ship.

While he was reading this statement to Commander Castle, translating it from Hebrew, Lieutenant-Colonel Efrat paused at one point to say that the Government of Israel had received a statement from the United States Government saying that *Liberty* had been identified six hours prior to the attack rather than one hour, as stated in an earlier US Government communication.

When he transmitted the details of his discussion with Colonel Efrat, Commander Castle wrote into his telegram the following comment: 'Lieutenant-Colonel Efrat probably noted the Naval Attaché's appearance of surprise and incredulity as he read off some of the above points. When he finished his reading he asked what the US Naval Attaché thought of the findings 'off the record'. The US Naval Attaché pretended he had not heard the question and thanked the Colonel for his time. The burden of diplomacy bore heavily on the US Naval Attaché.'

Commander Castle's evaluations were that (A), the IDF Navy Standing Order to attack any ship moving at more than 20 knots was incomprehensible; (B) two of the IDF justifications for their actions were mutually contradictory. First they had said that since the speed of the unidentified ship was as high as 30 knots, they could not have thought it was *Liberty*. Then they had said the ship was feasibly identified as *El Quseir*. *El Quseir* was rated with a maximum speed of only 14 knots, four less than *Liberty*. If the '30-knot ship' was not *Liberty* it followed that it also could not have been *El Quseir*; (C) it was difficult to accept that a professional naval officer of the rank of Commander could look at *Liberty* and think she was a 30-knot ship; (D) the smoke which covered *Liberty* and made her difficult to identify was a result of the IDF Air Force attack, so it could hardly be used as the Israelis were trying to use it, as an excuse that *Liberty* was throwing up a smoke screen to conceal her identity and was therefore an enemy ship.

Commander Castle closed his report with the remark that while walking to their cars Lieutenant-Colonel Efrat mentioned that General Rabin had never been so angry as when he read the current *Newsweek* magazine comment on the *Liberty* incident (*Newsweek* 19 June 1967, Periscope column said in part: 'High Washington officials believe the Israelis knew *Liberty*'s capabilities and that the attack might not have been accidental. One high level theory holds that someone in the Israeli armed forces ordered that *Liberty* be sunk because it had intercepted messages which revealed Israel had started the fighting'). Commander Castle replied that he took no notice of news media reporting on the incident. He did not indicate to Lieutenant-Colonel Efrat, who was obviously fishing for such an indication, that American intelligence had identified the 'someone in the Israeli armed forces' as the Israeli Defence Minister and Supreme Commander, General Moshe Dayan.

On 21 June 1967, the American Government was advised by the Israelis that the Israeli Judge Advocate had decided to hold an inquiry to determine if any individual should stand accountable for the attack. No such inquiry was ever held nor was an inquiry even initially convened and then postponed.

Chapter Six

Between the events immediately following the attack upon *Liberty* there occurred a minor and very private diplomatic and political furore.

Walt Rostow went to see the Chairman of the JCS and the Secretary of the Navy, and told them confidentially that it would be better if everyone forgot about the *Liberty* and let the State Department settle the tricky business of compensation and reparation from Israel in its own way. Also it would be better that no publicity or public statements be issued from the military.

The generals and the admirals in the Pentagon had been under constant fire from the politicians since the start of the Vietnam War and they were used to appeals for softness and pacifist ideals. They thought Johnson better than his predecessor, the late John F. Kennedy, but it would make little difference to their overall sentiments if he had presided under the Republican rather than the Democrat banner, he would have still been 'gutless' to the military. However, they did tolerate him, and occasionally they even thought of him as 'not too bad a guy'; this was mostly due to Rostow, since, on the advice of the ambitious and hawkish Security Adviser, Johnson had not only conceded to continuing the Vietnam War, he had agreed to escalate US offensive action, although not without trepidation.

The President was physically sick, mentally weary, and only nine months away from the collapse of health the Vietnam War would force on him; he did not have the strength of character or resolution to make firm, clear decisions on any important home or foreign policy without worrying himself into a state of deep, abject depression. Rostow had advised JFK on national security; Kennedy then considered the advice and made his own decisions. As Johnson's Security Adviser, Rostow told the President what to do and the President did it. While the military establishment were pleased enough that Rostow favoured all-out war in Vietnam, they did not trust his overall judgement on national security matters and resented the power he had. Overall, Rostow was not liked in the Pentagon or at the CIA although the Agency's Director, Richard Helms, and its head of Counter Intelligence, James Angleton, saw in the National Security Adviser a kindred, devious, hawkish spirit. Rostow believed he had control at the CIA because the CIA told him he had. However, he had more liaison with Agency activities than the Pentagon had, even though the Agency had officers sitting with the Joint Chiefs at all meetings. Richard Helms considered it his duty to pursue the policies of the CIA in foreign affairs, not the policies of the State Department, or even of the White House if this could be avoided. Helms was a professional. The President and his staff were amateurs. Helms and his men were not contemptuous without good reason. Like the military they saw politicians and their staff as 'gutless'. The amateurs were ill-informed and without the hard nerve needed to make decisions and perform acts for which there was no political charter. Helms and his CIA chiefs were makers of unethical policies. A CIA man of the time described those policies as 'unethical acts of covert diplomacy'. Whatever he may or may not have been, Richard Helms was not diplomatic but he was covert, so covert that in many instances only he and his chosen half-dozen at the Agency really knew what America was doing overseas. Helms thought that was definitely the best way to do it.

Since the start of the Vietnam War, the Agency and the military had cooperated after a fashion in coordinating straight military and special-service-group operations with overt Agency penetration. This was the case particularly in Laos and Cambodia where covert acts were carried out along with covert tactics in support, providing money, weapons, equipment and advisers to the anti-Communist factions. In fact they ran their Vietnam operation clearly and almost openly in respect of their cooperative role with the other command units of the US forces.

In other areas the field was not so clear and the operations were not so clean-cut. The darkest and most important in the long term, and the most rapidly changing field of operations, was in the Mediterranean, not just in the Middle East but the whole area which was undergoing violent political upheaval caused by increasing

Soviet penetration. The Agency were primarily concerned with the internal subversive effect which the Soviet penetration had encouraged against American interests. The military were more concerned with the growth of Soviet military power, particularly the continued increase in naval strength which they saw as building up to challenge NATO's domination of the Mediterranean. Before the 1967 Arab-Israeli War the Soviet Navy, lacking a Mediterranean fleet, showed only a minimal presence in the area. Immediately after the war and ever since, that presence has increased both in surface craft and submarines to become a significant threat to NATO.

In 1956 with the stepping-up of Soviet penetration in the Middle East, the CIA, which was very weak in an area formerly dominated only by British Intelligence, became interested in the operations of Mossad, the Israeli Intelligence Service (IIS), and agreed on a deal with the Israelis by which they would work as a combined unit, relying entirely upon IIS penetration of surrounding Arab countries for all intelligence relating to the area, including the Soviet presence in it. Following the abortive Anglo-Israeli operation in 1956 to take control of Sinai and the Suez Canal which resulted in a sharp exchange between President Eisenhower and the Government of David Ben Gurion, the CIA/IIS relations became more secretive and were detached from official US policy in the Middle East and were kept secret from the White House.

Forced to abandon Sinai at the demand of President Eisenhower, and once again fearful for her security with hostile Arabs on her doorstep, Israel extracted as a major part of her co-operation deal with the CIA (Angleton negotiating on the Agency's behalf) materials and technicians to help Israel develop her own nuclear weapons.

Angleton worked closely with the head of the IIS counter intelligence, Ephraim 'Eppy' Evron, the man in charge of all Mossad's covert operations, except those against former Nazi war criminals. Evron was to weave constantly in and out of American-Israeli scandals including the *Liberty* affair, in which he acted as deputy Israeli Ambassador in Washington.

Evron had pursued a policy within Mossad to bring about the total destruction of American détente with the Arab world, a lowering of tension which had started with Eisenhower, increased with Kennedy, but was now sinking with Johnson, mostly due to the influence of Walt Rostow.

James Angleton had encouraged a strong Israeli lobby in the US Government. He, personally, did not agree with détente strategy. But his own plans were rooted in virulent anti-Soviet feelings, not in any sentimental support for the Jewish State.

He considered the Arabs treacherous and too deep in the Soviet pocket. Israel represented the only anti-Soviet ally in the area who could be trusted and Israeli intelligence agents were the only people with the ethnic capabilities to effectively penetrate the enemy.

Angleton first became aware of Evron as an operator when he heard how Mossad's counter intelligence organizer had plotted a covert operation in Cairo to blow up the US Consulate, blame it on Nasser's nationalist supporters and so stir up a wave of anti-Arab sentiment in America. The mission fouled up. Nine Israeli agents were captured while laying the charges and were brought to trial by the Egyptians for sabotage. Two were executed, the rest were given long prison sentences.

Angleton learned that the circumstances surrounding the operation precluded any responsibility on Evron's part for the failure. Basically, the idea had been a good one. Angleton also admired the way Evron crawled out from the ruins of the affair after its failure and escaped without any of the mud of scandal sticking to him. The man who took the blame was Defence Minister Pinhal Lavon, the operation being subsequently dubbed the Lavon Affair.

In mid-July the USS *Liberty* returned home, slipping into the Navy yard at Norfolk, Virginia, quietly and without the ceremony she deserved for the heroic service she had performed. She was laid up in the yard for a time, then turned over to the Department of Commerce and shunted into their derelicts' fleet. In the summer of 1975 she was finally sold for scrap and was broken up. It was the symbolic end of an incident that many parties in Washington and Israel wished to forget.

But forgetting was not so easy. Voices had to be silenced in the Senate and questions dismissed in secret congressional hearings. The military were bound, although reluctantly, by security regulations. Commander McGonagle, awarded the Congressional Medal

73

of Honour for Gallantry and promoted Captain, was given a desk job at naval intelligence in Washington. President Johnson, under pressure from the Department of the Navy, awarded a General Citation to the ship. This was the Navy's way of giving *Liberty* her own medal, although as she was broken up it was something of an empty gesture.

With the breaking up of the ship the last evidence of the 1967 attack was scattered like dead ashes. The incident still lingered as an administrative issue in the State Department files, since damages of an estimated seven million dollars were still outstanding as 'material damage' to the United States Government from Israel. But absolutely nothing was being done about it and no correspondence over the issue had passed between the two governments since 1971. Everyone had conveniently forgotten *Liberty*, and Captain McGonagle had retired early to Santa Barbara, California, because of the lingering effects of wounds sustained during the attack. From an official viewpoint the matter was buried. But in November 1975 I arrived in Washington, more than curious about the events behind *Liberty*'s attack and determined to resurrect the corpse.

Chapter Seven

The reporter's part in the affair, my part, began in the spring of 1975, just before *Liberty* was broken up for scrap.

At the time I saw it only as a faint possibility. I thought on the whole it probably added up to not much more than a mediocre tale of war and heroes. It was the sort of story I would never have troubled myself with if I had owned some better property. But I owned nothing and was thankful for anything.

The circumstances of the *Liberty* incident were related to me in Doha Qatar by an American film producer, Tito de Nagy Howard. I had met him early in April in the lobby of the Intercontinental Hotel in Dubai. When he discovered I was an investigative journalist and that I was considered by the PLO to be 'pro-Palestinian' he eagerly gave me an idea, to resurrect the *Liberty* incident as a whole new story. It was an idea he had been carrying around for a long time. In its original time, he said, it had been suppressed. So far only the bare bones of it had been exposed but there was much, much more.

It was easy to make friends with Tito Howard. He was unusual, even for an American. His father's family tree went back to the English Howards of Norfolk, he claimed, while on his mother's side Cherokee-Indian and Slavic blood were mixed. Born in New York thirty-six years before, he had been raised in the heart of Dixie, and his southern 'rebel's' outlook combined with his stylish appearance to form a man whose individuality made an immediate appeal.

When I was introduced to him he was fresh from a High Court battle in London where the Government of Israel had tried to obtain an injunction to prevent him distributing a documentary film called 'Kuneitra – Death of a City', shot on the Golan Heights in Syria. Howard had won his case and was now riding high through the Arab world on the euphoria of his legal victory.

He wished to follow up his Kuneitra film with other similar material. He was looking for any propagandist subject for another indictment of the Israeli State. The story of the USS *Liberty* was, to his mind, just this sort of material. He believed that the attack on the ship had been premeditated and deliberate, but all he had were theories. Beyond the bare outline of the story he had so far been unable to extract anything from its complex and yet unknown background. Sometime in the future he said he intended to make a documentary film examining and explaining the incident. He had been working on it for a long time. He believed the Israeli action in trying to suppress his Kuneitra film had been part of an overall campaign to destroy his credibility as an independent film producer who recognized the legitimacy of the Arab cause. He said that the Israelis had heard he was investigating *Liberty* and wanted to stop him doing so.

His war with them went back a long way. Along with his normal business activities, which included a country and western club called 'Tito's', he supported a local radio station which had been established to help promote understanding for the problems of dispossessed Palestinians. In 1973 'Tito's' was burnt to the ground. The police established the fire as arson and blamed rival nightclub owners. Howard denied this. He claimed the fire had been started by 'Zionist agents' trying to bankrupt him and destroy his work for the Palestinian cause and his plans to expose what he called 'the Zionist conspiracy in America'. The *Liberty* story was the cornerstone in his exposure campaign of this so-called Zionist conspiracy and he wanted to tell the American people through the story of the *Liberty* that the Zionists they financed repaid their loyalty and trust by acts of war against the very people who were their backers and their friends.

I had heard all this sort of thing before. Impartiality was perhaps the main problem in writing about Middle East affairs and I was not sure that I possessed such a fragile virtue. I was certain very few of my contemporaries did. Most of them supported the Israeli view for the practical reason that the proprietors of their newpapers took a political stand in favour of Israel. In the United States this was natural enough, since the wealth of the media and the film industry was very much founded on Jewish money. Those journalists who were pro-Arab were usually politically far left and often supported other international revolutionary themes which had no rational connection with the Arab-Israeli conflict. I found both pro-Israeli and pro-Arab commentators much alike: they were usually disagreeable, bombastic and not really very convincing. Tito Howard was an exception. Despite his very radical pro-Arab stance, he was a generous, charming and often very persuasive man.

I returned to London towards the end of May and worked hard but unsuccessfully on various projects until I met Bob Guccione, the publisher of *Penthouse* magazine, in August. He was looking for ideas for investigative political stories and when I showed him the synopsis of the *Liberty* piece he agreed to finance an investigation into its background. I accepted the commission, but my enthusiasm for the story was then still subdued.

I started immediately on the basic research, reading books on the Six Day War, the cuttings from newspapers and magazines; and I made interminable phone calls to the Foreign Office, the Ministry of Defence, the Israeli Embassy, the American Embassy, the Arab embassies, willing to listen to anyone who might give me a line on the USS *Liberty*. The first significant thing I noticed was that very little existed on the circumstances surrounding the attack beyond the basic news stories which said it had happened and that there had been casualties. When Tito Howard first mentioned the story I reacted with my reporter's instinctive curiosity. Since the attack could never have been the mistake the Israelis claimed – even a half-witted civilian could have recognized *Liberty* as a US Navy ship by her identification numbers and her cut – then it must have been deliberate and premeditated; so why . . ?

This journalist's instinct was no stronger than average but it responded particularly to one question. It was not directly concerned with the circumstances of the attack, but with its aftermath. In 1967 the *Liberty* story should have been a sensation in the United States but no one bothered to follow it up. Why had there been no big in-depth piece in the *Washington Post* or the *New York Times*? The only challenging pieces I could find were in the Periscope column of *Newsweek* of 14 June and in the 28 July issue of Zorepath (New Jersey) *Herald of Freedom*, a Republican newspaper notorious for its extreme right-wing views.

The *Newsweek* piece claimed the Israelis deliberately attacked and tried to destroy *Liberty* because the spy ship had evidence Israel had started the war at a time when the Israelis were claiming the Arabs had started it.

The *Herald of Freedom* piece was based upon a declassified transcript of the Court of Inquiry which had just been released and which contained Admiral Kidd's finding that while the US Navy had to accept Israel's apology, it did not accept the explanation for the attack, which was of mistaken identity. In sifting through possible reasons for the attack, the newspaper suggested it was all probably to do with General Moshe Dayan, the hawkish Israeli Defence Minister.

The only other significant item of question-raising was by the syndicated columnist Jack Anderson, who asked about *Liberty*'s role as a spy ship, expressed the opinion that the attack was no accident and exposed the fact that initial congressional hearings on the matter were held totally in secret, were unusually leakproof and that there was a lot of friction over this issue on the Hill.

The strange lack of interest in the press puzzled me. When it was still fresh the story was good by international standards and fantastic as an American 'home' news item, putting a powerful local slant on the Middle East War.

The lack of interest went further. In his memoirs 'The Vantage Point', written in 1971 – four years after the *Liberty* incident – Lyndon Johnson remembered the attack had left 'ten dead and one hundred wounded'. It was a strange lapse of memory even for Johnson under the strain which had already started to crack him apart emotionally.

It was this sort of initial discovery of research which kept firing my curiosity. Enthusiasm was building up for the story.

Then there were little titbits like CIA staffer Patrick McGarvey's claim in his book 'CIA – The Myth and the Madness' that, after hearing about the *Liberty* attack, the Joint Chiefs of Staff had called for an airstrike on the Israeli torpedo-boat base at Haifa and that this order had to be countermanded by presidential intervention.

When I read this I decided there would surely be some old crotchety general officers around in the Pentagon who were still carrying a grudge over the *Liberty* and would be glad to help reopen an inquiry about it to give the Israelis the comeuppance they deserved, even after eight years.

There were also references in a number of books and articles to the Rostow brothers, Eugene and Walt, respectively Under Secretary of State for Near Eastern Affairs and Assistant Adviser to the President on national security. Commentators had doubts about their motives of involvement. One of the most serious doubts raised against the Rostows was their involvement in Zionist fund-raising activities with Arthur Goldberg, the US Government's United Nations Security Council representative. But these allegations were levelled mostly by pro-Arab writers like Mohammed Heikal, editor of the Cairo daily *Al Akram*. As public figures in the US Jewish community it was not irregular for the Rostows and Goldberg to raise funds for Israel. However, I did feel that in view of his obvious pro-Jewish bias it was a poor and suspect appointment to have Eugene Rostow as Under Secretary of State for Foreign Affairs 'East of Suez'. I also felt that Goldberg must have been uncomfortably embarrassed trying to promote a ceasefire at the UN which, if it had been implemented on time, would have prevented the Israeli attack and the capture and occupation of Arab land which was vital to Israeli security and which has now become the crux of all Middle Eastern wranglings.

Tito Howard kept on telling me this was part of the Zionist conspiracy. I agreed the Rostow/Goldberg appointments were suspect but I could not accept the contention they were part of 'a Zionist plot'. This constant haranguing about Zionist plots, together with the hours I spent reading up the subject of the Six Day War, was nearly enough to wear down all my enthusiasm and end my inquiries.

Two things saved the story. One was the promise made by an American banker friend in London, that he could secure an interview for me with Bill Mittendorf, the Secretary for the Navy in Washington. The other was a quite coincidental affair which had nothing to do with the *Liberty* but a lot to do with Tito Howard.

Just before getting the *Liberty* story commission from Guccione I had moved into an apartment in Cheyne Place, Chelsea. This became a handy base for Howard while he was in transit between the United States and the Middle East.

At the same time Howard was making a film in Syria about that country's Jewish community and how, contrary to Israeli propaganda, they had full civil rights and were under no social restraint. The film was directed by a mutual friend of ours, Peter Griffith, a completely apolitical animal.

Griffith and his wife Marlena spent some weeks with Tito Howard in Syria and Lebanon and, on their return to London, they told me they had met a strange friend of Howard's called Harry Fischer.

Harry Fischer, born thirty-four years earlier in Paris, as Henri, now commuted between homes in Sydney, Paris and Los Angeles. He was a multi-millionaire business executive, owning a chain of health farms in Australia and America, a film production company in Los Angeles and, as a personal interest, a Palestinian newspaper in Australia. He did not smoke or drink. He was a vegetarian and a health and exercise fanatic.

When Fischer's name was first mentioned it was only in idle conversation about the Syrian trip and Howard's Syrian/Jewish film. Howard was staying with a friend in Fulham, in south-west London, and was so secretive about exactly where his lodgings were that he would not tell me the name of the road or the number of the house. We always arranged to meet in a pub in the centre of Fulham, about twenty minutes' drive from my apartment. He constantly implied that he was being pursued and that his very life was in danger. When he arrived in London, he said, he had quickly noticed he was under surveillance. A man followed him everywhere. He had been unable to go to his Fulham address and had had to stay in a different hotel every day for three days. On the third day, he had lost his pursuer at Russell Square Underground station by the old trick of travelling on the down escalator then immediately running back up the other one.

That night he came to my apartment and placed a phone call to a number in Singapore. When the call finally came through Howard had a very brief conversation with a woman who was apparently a secretary. She told him to call at the Qantas office in London and collect an air ticket to Melbourne via Hong Kong, where he was to stop off for a meeting.

He told me the man he had to see was 'a guy who might put

up big bread for some of our film projects. He owns one of the biggest post-production companies in the States.' After the Far East trip, he said he had to go to the Middle East, to Baghdad, and then he would come back through London on his way to the States.

The following day at 2 a.m. a call came through to my number from Singapore. It was for Tito Howard from 'a Mr Fischer'. I told the caller, a woman, that Tito was not available right now and would Mr Fischer return the call. She said yes, it would be returned at midnight.

I contacted Howard at his Soho film cutting room and he came round to my apartment at about ten that night. At midnight the call came through. He took it on the bedroom extension and spoke for about fifteen minutes. He then told me he had to leave the next day for Hong Kong.

Afterwards I drove him to Fulham, setting him down at the corner of Munster Road and the New King's Road.

When I got back to my apartment, I noticed that he had scrawled a note and his ballpoint pen had dug through to the blotter pad underneath. It read 'Ring Iraqis over Whitlam loan'. There was also a phone number for the Iraqi Embassy in London. 'Whitlam' was probably Gough Whitlam, the Australian Labour Prime Minister. It was not too common a name and Tito Howard's business did have Australian connections. The last word, 'loan', put the rest of the message into some sort of perspective. Gough Whitlam's Government was in serious trouble over repeated scandals in the Australian press alleging he had accepted multi-million-dollar loans of Arab money to help bolster Australia's diving economy. The previous year, on 13 December, 1974, the Executive Council agreed an authorization for the Government to borrow $4 thousand million overseas. Whitlam's Government began to raise the money using backdoor intermediaries who went around the Middle East organizing loans from Arab countries on the strength of Whitlam's pro-Arab policies. One of these intermediaries was Harry Fischer. Another was Philip Cairns, son of Whitlam's deputy, Dr Jim Cairns. It was alleged that one of the deals allowed Philip Cairns to take a commission of $600,000 on a loan raised in Saudi Arabia of $2 million. Cairns allegedly

81

split his commission with a business partner and a London financier.

At the time Tito Howard and Peter Griffith met Harry Fischer in August-September, the Cairns-Whitlam scandal was still fresh and was being pursued by reporters from the Melbourne *Age*, one of the newspapers owned by the press baron, Rupert Murdoch. According to Howard, Fischer knew Murdoch and had told Howard that Murdoch was a deadly enemy of Whitlam and was determined to destroy him at all costs.

Thinking about this, I remembered Tito Howard saying that Rupert Murdoch had wanted to buy the *Liberty* story – or at least the basic fact synopsis which was all Tito had – for '$20,000 plus expenses'. I thought this was a very extravagant offer for a story which was then eight years old and had nothing new to revive it. Howard had also said Harry Fischer was a good friend of the Murdochs and because of this friendship, Fischer was able to secure an introduction for Howard to sell his story to Murdoch. Whether Murdoch offered $20,000 because he was interested in *Liberty* or just because he wanted to buy into Tito Howard, only Murdoch knew.

The whole Fischer, Whitlam, Murdoch triangle was full of paradoxical involvements. Fischer was dealing amicably with Murdoch while the press baron was trying to kill Whitlam's Government with the scandals publicized in his newspapers. Simultaneously, Fischer was supposedly trying to bolster Whitlam with Arab money – the very thing Murdoch was criticizing Whitlam for. The whole business was not just tangled – it was positively bizarre. And flitting in and out of it in the role of intermediary and general helpmate was Tito Howard.

At this stage I was not even indirectly involved. Over the next few days I researched the background to the loans scandal and tried to research Fischer. I came up with nothing. The man's daily life was shrouded in mystery and silence.

I was just about at the point where I had decided to abandon my inquiries into the Australian business when I received a call from a friend at the Foreign Office, a man I had known during his colonial police service in Kenya. He invited me to have lunch with him.

Over the port my friend came to the point. He said he had heard

I was inquiring into the Whitlam/Arab-loans business and that I knew an American – he did say American – called Harry Fischer. I told him I didn't know Harry Fischer, only his friend Tito Howard.

'Well,' my friend said, 'we would be grateful if you would drop the whole matter. It is complicated and, because of Australia's position in the Commonwealth, could be embarrassing to HMG. If you agree to drop the issue I think we can more than help you on the *Liberty* thing.'

'Like what sort of help?' I asked.

'Well, I know the case officer who was involved in the main intelligence operation for MI6 during the Six Day War. In December he is going to Nairobi on leave from the Gulf where he is serving a secondment to one of the local armies. I will contact him and tell him to give you all the help you need.'

'And in return you want me to drop the Australian dossier?' I didn't tell him I barely had a dossier, only a lot of good hunches.

'Yes. I know you don't have much' – he knew so I wasn't so smart after all – 'but it's just better you don't pursue it. Can we shake hands on the deal?'

'Sure. I've nothing to lose. As you quite rightly say, I have very little and I doubt if I could get much more. Australia is not in my scene of operations. The *Liberty* is my prime target. From my side it's an excellent agreement.'

'Good. I'll ring you later this week with the details of the chap you can meet in Nairobi. Meanwhile, I should get your employer to send you to Washington and you can ring these two chaps' – he gave me two telephone numbers in Falls Church, Virginia – 'who are connected with the State Department–Central Intelligence Agency thing. I will speak to them first – they are both friends of mine – and ask them to give you the background to exactly why the Americans found it necessary to use a spy ship against Israel. I frankly don't think they will tell you too much but if you analyse their information carefully it might help you to start piecing your story together.'

I did not even try to speculate as to why British Intelligence should want to keep the Whitlam business out of the newspapers, or what their interest in Mr H. Fischer was.

Perhaps if I had been a staffman on a newspaper it would have been different. As a staffman with a regular salary you could afford to uphold the (supposed) high ideals of your profession and have no fear or favour for anyone, including your own Government. For a freelance things were different. First of all, I had no financial incentive to tackle the Australian story. Secondly, it involved Rupert Murdoch, and I did not want to find myself on the wrong side of one of the world's biggest newpaper proprietors. Third and last, I didn't want to upset my own government. My position, without the back-up of a newspaper organization, was precarious to say the least. If the Foreign Office or Intelligence, or whoever they were, wanted to help me in exchange for my forgetting Australia, Whitlam, Fischer, Murdoch and any other part of the plot, that was fine by me. I left the restaurant feeling cheerful and optimistic that I had a real chance of plugging together the *Liberty* story.

Chapter Eight

I slept off the food and wine and awoke lying on the candlewick bedspread of my large double bed staring at the white-washed ceiling of the bedroom. It was dancing with shadows. The traffic was heavy in Royal Hospital Road and the curtains were not pulled against the headlights and the traffic noise.

I changed from my blue shirt and pin-stripe suit into old Levi's, heavy denim shirt and brown cowboy boots, my everyday clothes. The lounge window was open and the breeze from the river just across the Chelsea Embankment was shaking the Vietnamese windbell hanging from the curtain-rail. It reminded me of Saigon.

I was still full from lunch but decided it was time to go out for the ceremony of dinner even though I wasn't really hungry. It was now 8 p.m. I lounged back and watched the headlights flickering across the high rococo-patterned white ceiling. I hated being alone in the city. In the country I was always looking for solitude, but never felt lonely. In the city when I sat alone I let my imagination run away with me. Perhaps I should ask my friend at MI6 for some sort of support, a back-up as the Americans would say.

I got up and walked across to the window. The apartment was on the third floor of an old Georgian house. You could see across the Chelsea Botanical Gardens to the river where the rising tide flowed under the line of lights along the Embankment. Across the river you could see the fairy lights of Battersea Park and the Albert Bridge. It was all so tranquil it made me think that this was how the real world should be.

Since the Jordanian civil war of 1970 I had done a lot of war reporting. I did it because it was easy. Sometimes the excitement was stimulating and interesting, but basically it was just very easy. There was no effort involved in collecting the day-to-day material for good copy. It was possible to achieve literary heroism without moving out of the hotel bar. This often happened. I had acquired experience as a bar hero as I had in every other field of foreign correspondents' combat. I had a firm idea that one day I would write a biographical novel. But the future seemed always to convert too quickly into the past and the book was now many years behind schedule. Occasionally I would sit down and type the first paragraph of the first chapter. Sometimes I would get as much as a thousand words onto three or four pages. Then it ended. The war correspondent role was just one part of my jaded literary ambition.

When the Middle East war of 1973 broke out it came almost as divine inspiration. I had been slack for a long time and suddenly I was moving again.

I was assigned to the war by the *Manchester Evening News*. I filled my canvas kitbag with a helmet, canteen, ammunition belts to carry films and all the paraphernalia of soldiering, and marched to the front on an El Al 707 from London and a hire car from Avis, Tel Aviv. I put a well-thumbed and earmarked copy of John Steinbeck's 'Once there was a War' into my kitbag for good measure.

During the days that followed I saw my share of action. Most often I was with Israeli troops. By changing fronts and sides I also saw combat with Arab guerillas, Arab regulars and Arab refugees; I argued with border guards, embassy officials, censors and airline personnel. The core of my work, although I rarely thought about it until a long time afterwards, comprised most frequently senseless arguing with minor ministers, officials, information men and telex operators. My most repeated theme in cables to Brian Redhead, my editor, was a plea for more expenses money to be wired to Thomas Cook's or Barclays Bank. My most enduring memories of war travels were of the bars I sat in when the fighting was over. These were the places which helped you to appreciate your own sense of high drama and noble composure. You were always the real battle-worn hero, impressing the pretty girls with your expense account and your tall tales. The soldiers, alive, dead or maimed, were only copy fodder. Occasionally I did feel ashamed of my cynicism but I rarely tried to suppress it. It was all part of being a correspondent.

I often sat at night in the window of my apartment watching the river and thinking about myself like this. Once I left my apartment and started walking briskly along Royal Hospital Road I stopped philosophizing. The fresh wind cleared my head.

After dinner, over coffee, I worked at the notes I had made so far on *Liberty*. I liked to work in restaurants. The bustling atmosphere remined me of the busy newspaper offices where I had spent the most useful part of my working life. When I left the restaurant at 1 a.m. I had worked on almost sixty pages of *Liberty* notes. Outside it was raining a fine drizzle. I walked along the King's Road for a while, staring into the winter-bright shop windows, then I cut down Flood Street to Cheyne Place.

In the apartment I switched on the small reading-lamp beside my desk and opened my notebook. On one page, while I was doodling in the restaurant, I had drawn a diagram. It was a triangle. *Liberty* was at the apex and Israel and America at each corner of the base. Mid-way along the base I had placed a cross. Jordan was written above it. This was a thesis. It was the device I had formulated to help me understand and explain the complex nature of America's Middle Eastern role. I kept turning over in my mind an interview I had seen on BBC television between King Hussein and Ludovic Kennedy, in which the King had said his long rift with President Nasser was very firmly based on the way he had been mis-informed by Egypt of events during the Six Day War. The King had said that Nasser deliberately misled him about the progress being made by Egyptian troops. This encouraged the Jordanians to miscalculate their own strategic position totally. It resulted in heavy losses of manpower and materials.

From the documents and reports I had studied so far I knew that Hussein, in his honest attempts to find a working solution to the problem of the presence of Israel, had cooperated very closely with the United States and that he had discussed his security affairs with the CIA. There was nothing sinister in this. He had to choose between Russia and America; he chose America. At the same time, the American relationship with Israel could be described as better than cordial. The Americans had their feet firmly set in both camps. To play a double role effectively they needed to keep a close watch on both sides, and America's eye on the Six Day War was *Liberty*. The ship was monitoring Israeli activity because the US Government believed the Israelis were in process of doing or were about to do something of which they did not approve.

The sequence of events which led to the attack on *Liberty* could

87

be set out in the following order: first, a series of shuttle diplomatic moves between Israel and Washington, Egypt and Washington and then Washington and Israel; second, a series of secret meetings between the State Department and King Hussein in which the King was promised he would be protected by the United States from 'Israeli aggression'; third, these diplomatic moves were suddenly complicated by President Nasser's military manoeuvres during May, starting with the closure of the Straits of Tiran. Exactly what Nasser finally intended to do was vague. When he mobilized the Egyptian forces in Sinai even his general staff did not quite understand his full motives for doing so. They assumed that sooner or later he intended to make an attack on the Israelis. The Israelis pre-empted any Egyptian military action by making their own strike on 5 June.

The day war began, the USS *Liberty* arrived off Gaza; three days later, she was attacked by Israeli planes and warships. Then the fighting ended and Israel was in command of a large segment of strategically important Arab territory which it still holds and which is still in dispute.

Looking at the basic facts, I decided that I should start my detailed investigation with a list of questions compiled from them. These were:

1. Going right back to 1963 when American Middle East policy became a serious issue for the Kennedy administration, why were so many people opposed to John F. Kennedy's initiative in the Middle East which played heavily on improving American relations with the Arab world in general and with Egypt in particular?

2. When the initiative collapsed with JFK's assassination in Dallas why was it left until barely forty-eight hours before the Six Day War began before an attempt was started to reach a diplomatic compromise between Egypt and America? It seemed more than just a coincidence that the Israelis attacked Egypt almost immediately a public announcement was made that the Egyptian Vice-President Zakaria Mohieddin was to visit Washington and Vice President Hubert Humphrey was to visit Cairo for the opening of new talks designed to avoid confrontation.

3. If there was such a close rapport with King Hussein immediately before hostilities broke out, and the tone of these

1 The USS *Liberty* showing some of the radio masts but without the 'big ear' sonar

2 Commander (now Captain, retired) William McGonagle. He is wearing the
Congressional Medal of Honour he received for his heroism during the attack

3 Israeli Mirage fighters making an attack run aimed at knocking out the ship's communication antennae

4 Israeli MTB's making the attack run which delivered the fatal torpedo into *Liberty*'s communications room

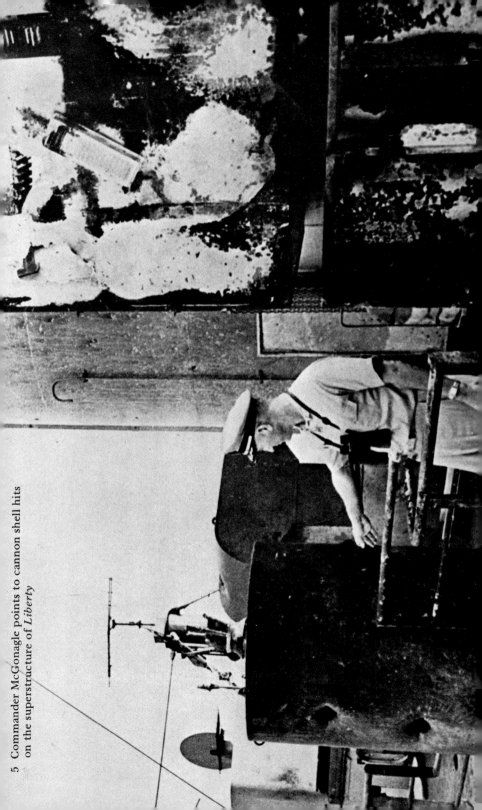

5 Commander McGonagle points to cannon shell hits on the superstructure of *Liberty*

6 The torpedo hit which wiped out *Liberty*'s communications room and almost sank her

Israeli Mirage jets on patrol

8 The nuclear-powered fleet ballistic missile submarine, the USS *Andrew Jackson*

Jordanian-American relationships was known to Israeli intelligence, why did the Israelis make such a desperate effort to capture and occupy Jordanian territory, knowing this would cause a serious rift between Hussein and the West? Or did they do it knowing they would create such a rift?

4. How much information did America have in respect of Israel's strike plans? If they were in possession of enough pre-war planning to dispatch the USS *Liberty* from the West African coast to the Egyptian coast to arrive almost on the day the war started, why could they not have used their information to pressure Israel away from a military confrontation with the Arabs and so not allow war to take place at all?

5. Since the whole pre-planning of the Israeli strike against Egypt smelt so obviously of a Washington/Tel Aviv plot, who and what was behind such a plot and what was the final intention?

I studied these questions and then began to make first answers to them from the top of my head.

Opposition to an American/Arab initiative lay historically in the hands of the powerful Jewish lobby in the US Government. It was possible to throw out plenty of names, but could any of the pro-Israel people have been actively working against an improvement in US/Arab relations knowing that to jeopardize such an improvement would provide a serious setback to US foreign policy?

The biggest supporters of Israeli political and military deals in the Middle East at that time were in the CIA. It had already been shown on numerous occasions that the CIA not only often refused to agree with State Department policy when it conflicted with its own but actually worked to its own ends, overriding official policy if necessary. There were plenty of rumours circulating about the 1950s' deals in which the CIA secretly provided technicians and materials for the Israelis to develop nuclear reactor sites in the Negev Desert in contravention the wishes of both the western powers and the Soviet Union. Breaking this particular plot down to personalities, it was well known that the head of CIA counter intelligence, James Angleton, had hated President Eisenhower. Angleton thought Harry Truman's recognition of Israel had been heroic and Eisenhower's attempt to prevent the Arabs slipping deeper into the Russian camp by virtually taking their side was a waste of time and a sell-out to America's Jewish friends.

Eisenhower had been one of the principal objectors to Truman's initial recognition of Israel. At the time the General had told the President: 'Recognizing this State is to sow the seeds for a crisis in the area that can only ever be resolved by all-out war . . .along with total loss of US prestige with the Arabs. Realistically they have everything we need, they have everything to offer. Israel has nothing to give us but trouble. Backing Israel, we are, in military terms, backing the wrong side.'

Inside the State Department the professional employees of government agreed with this view. So did most of the senior officers in the three services. The CIA were the only government 'professionals' at odds with the Eisenhower logic. They always seemed to be at odds with every President and his politics. Their theatre of war was located against many enemies, but the nucleus of these enemies was always Russia. The CIA counter intelligence view was 'Ignore the military and the State Department, we want to do our own thing.' In their minds full of Red Menace paranoia they were prepared to stamp on every obstacle.

If they were going to hurt the Russians in their biggest growth area, it was necessary to take sides with the only logical allies there. Britain and France had already tried this when Anthony Eden and Mendès-France committed themselves to an airborne attack on Egypt to seize the Suez Canal and overthrow Nasser. They were backed by an Israeli strike into Sinai.

Following the aftermath of Suez, as the western allies moved out and the Israelis left Sinai, the Russians moved in bringing arms and technicians and whole batteries of offensive long-range missiles for the Egyptians to point at Israel.

The control of Egyptian Government by the Russian KGB grew so strong in this period that it continued until well after Nasser's death. Everyone knew that the area head of Russian intelligence was Sami Sheraf, Nasser's personal adviser. He held an identical post to Walt Rostow's. He was also a colonel in the KGB. Rostow had only attended MIT.

Taking this as a measure of Russia's offensive intentions and deeply concerned over Soviet control of the Egyptian Government, CIA counter intelligence undertook on its own initiative to covertly help the Israelis. Angleton, on his personal initiative, virtually gave them atomic bombs and warheads, by providing a creative nuclear potential.

The rights and wrongs of this policy were a matter for conjecture. Angleton, as head of CIA counter intelligence, needed to try to redress the balance of power in the area. It was his job to fight Russians. The Russians were expanding their Middle East military potential. It could only be countered by the Americans creating their own, bigger, military potential. Logically, no matter how many powerful weapons the Arabs acquired with Russian aid and technical advice, they could never equal Israeli military power so long as Israel could match them in military technology. This meant Israel needed nuclear power.

But even this only worked as an ultimate deterrent. In conventional war Russian arms technology could favour the Arabs, if used efficiently. This was to be proven during the early stages of the October war. Everyone saw and remembered the power of the Russian Sams. On just one day on the Golan I counted twenty Israeli Phantoms and Skyhawks knocked out of the sky by Syrian/Russian Sam-6 missiles between daybreak and mid-morning.

Angleton believed he was right. His Agency backed his plan for covert Israeli nuclear power even though it was against the US Government's official policy which refused to give them missiles when the Israelis argued they needed them for their defence at a crucial time.

Covert US policy was aimed to bolster Israel, to the detriment of the Arabs and to generally confuse the Russians in the vital eastern Mediterranean strategic theatre, a policy many officers in NATO must have privately applauded. In fact it was gradually becoming apparent that it was almost unnecessary.

In 1967 Nasser was still in deep with the Russians but was beginning to make overtures to the West. His attitude suggested he was becoming both disenchanted by and afraid of increasing Russian control and interference in his country. Paradoxically this created suspicion on both sides. The US security agencies thought Nasser was playing a double game. He proved them right, in their view, when he ordered the blockade of the Straits of Tiran on 22 May.

With hindsight it now seems almost certain that a pre-emptive Israeli strike helped US counter intelligence to destroy any State Department plans to deal with Nasser and simultaneously ruined any plan of Nasser's to play a double game with the US in order to help him renegotiate his relationship with Russia.

This brought me back to the relations between Hussein and the USA. The King had enjoyed good relations with America ever since he took over the throne of Jordan from his father, a year after his grandfather's assassination in 1951. One of the things that worried him most of all was the growth of Arab nationalism promoted by the Russo-Egyptian alliance. His worries drove him to agree readily to help America bring an end to Nasserism and Russian influence in the Middle East if that was at all possible.

The flaw in Hussein's thinking appeared to be the too detailed knowledge the Israelis had of US/Jordanian relations and agreements. One could guess with some certainty that Mossad were well penetrated into Jordanian intelligence and were getting more than their fair share of intelligence returns on the Jordanians from the CIA.

Whatever the relationships may have been between Washington and Amman, the Israelis were quite prepared to say 'to hell with them' for two important reasons: Jerusalem and the strategically valuable West Bank of the River Jordan. If the war was to be fought it would probably give the Israelis their only chance of capturing these objectives, whether Washington wished them to or not. It was logical to assume the Israelis were working to their own independent aims even if these should contravene overall US planning for the area. So far as Israel was concerned, relations between Washington and Hussein as a bridge into the Arab world simply did not come into their reckoning. The Zionist principle was: look to yourself and your brothers.

I worked these lines of research until almost 5 a.m. I marked off passages in various books and magazine articles which supported my thesis and drew a calendar of events which were to be my scenario of Israeli/American and American/Arab relations over almost two decades, 1956 to 1975, the vital years. Then I went to bed.

At 10 a.m. I phoned the Waterloo contact number of my

Foreign Office friend and asked for another meeting.

'OK,' he said. 'Lobby of the Cumberland Hotel at one.'

We both arrived exactly on the hour. My friend was always punctual. He had been a soldier, a policeman or a civil servant his whole life. He looked exactly that. He was tall and thin, wore a toothbrush moustache, a black pin-stripe suit with narrow trouser legs and turn-ups and a finely-striped blue shirt with a deep-red tie, printed with a motif of gold crowns above an Arabic numeral three. As young men we had been members of a regiment in Africa. You rarely saw the tie these days. It belonged to a world gone by.

We were old enough friends to get quickly to the point. I said: 'I watched an interview between King Hussein and Ludovic Kennedy on BBC TV a few nights ago. Hussein was talking about the bitterness he felt over the lack of communication with Nasser during the '67 War. He suggested the information given to him by Nasser was detrimental to the Jordanian handling of the war. He suggested that Nasser relayed a totally false impression of the Egyptian handling of the situation after the initial Israeli strike. I thought about it last night in greater detail, did a bit of swotting and came to the conclusion it was all a little too pat to be a coincidence.'

The man wearing the King's African Rifles tie drew on his cigarette for a few moments. He wrinkled his moustache from side to side. It was a habit he had when he was thinking.

'What's your view?' he said. 'How about purely an old soldier's view. What would you have thought in the old days?'

I liked the question. I liked the certainty implicit in the reference to the old days.

'Cooking?' I said.

'Yes. Probably, anyway.'

'The Israelis had electronic radio-wave cooking facilities?'

'Personally, I can't say for sure, but the Ministry of Defence were aware that the Americans had developed highly sophisticated radio-wave interference and redirectional equipment in the 1960s, and the Israelis had been given this equipment as part of their agreement to act as the eyes of the CIA in the Middle East.'

'Could you provide me with documentary proof of this?'

'Don't be stupid. It's all still classified and I shouldn't really be telling you about it. We were not directly involved and our primary interest at the time lay in southern Arabia, not in the Arab-Israeli conflict at all except when we were coerced as one of the superpowers to add our support to American efforts. Our interest and involvement in Jordan in 1967 was subsidiary to American interest, except that we did have more actual working influence there than the Yanks. We still advised on military and intelligence matters. King Hussein dealt with the Americans because their coffers were always pretty full, but he respected us. I think he was both very angry and disenchanted when the Americans let the Jews overrun his territory after they had promised he would be safe from Israeli military conquest.

'The *Liberty* incident, the thing you are investigating, seemed to have a lot to do with the plans the Israelis had for Jordan which were being carried out without American knowledge or consent. The *Liberty* presence was part of an American show. It was being operated by the CIA jointly with naval intelligence. Of course it was an operation which did not concern us. To get some sort of an understanding of it you would need to get a look at some of the American intelligence briefings for '67. You also need to know a lot more about the American involvement with Israel and Jordan. Everyone knows the Israelis hit the bloody ship and it wasn't any accident. But all the loose facts need gluing together. Whatever you produce the Israelis are going to deny as a matter of course. It is the sort of secretive affair you are going to find hard to prove beyond the possibility of doubt.'

I nodded and he continued, 'I honestly don't know whether the CIA is aware of the extent of HMG's knowledge of the secret background to the '67 war although we do cooperate reasonably with them and they were fairly honest about it, cock-ups included. But you know what our relationship with Langley is like so I can't give you anything in the way of documentary evidence. Whatever you do publicly you do alone. As far as we are concerned you have no contact with us. Remember when you go to Washington that the CIA are just about as tough a gang as there are in the business, not excluding Mossad and the KGB. I suppose all intelligence agencies are pretty bad, but the CIA have the biggest resources to make themselves the toughest gang. There is still some bad feeling in our service over the lack of American cooperation in the '73

94

war. Sometimes they try to keep us in ignorance of their more devious plans.

'I will tell you just one more thing although it has nothing to do with *Liberty* in particular. Just think about the situation of the 1973 war and you will see it was almost the Six Day War in reverse, and it was cocked-up again to such an extent that the Americans put their military on Defence Condition Three, which is the first alert for a world stand-to, to prepare for a full confrontation with the Soviets.'

'What about the chances of approaching some of the people in Washington you told me about yesterday?'

'They're all right. They'll help a bit. But I think you are best dealing inside the military. They have little love for the IDF or the IIS. What I suggest you do is take the basic idea of what I have passed over to you, get your hard confirmation of it from Washington if you can, and then you will be well briefed to see the chap in Nairobi. You know the form. Play one lot off against the other. The Yanks get verbal diarrhoea with the press if you get them in the right mood at the right time. Try Admiral Fluckey or Vice-Admiral Rufus Taylor, and even Angleton if you can get at him. Taylor may or may not be a good bet. He was Deputy Director at the CIA when Helms was the boss and he had special responsibility for naval operations. Try General Brown at the Pentagon. He is Chairman of the Joint Chiefs and has a bee in his bonnet over American-Israeli military cooperation. Try Dean Rusk too. He was Secretary of State at the time and handled the *Liberty* affair. If you can get him in the mood he could tell you all about the people inside the administration who used their influence on President Johnson.'

'What was the Foreign Office's assessment of Johnson?'

'Officially it was very cordial, although Harold Wilson thought Johnson was an intellectual dwarf and a bit of a hick. Unofficially, the professionals in the FO felt sorry for the man because he should never have been pushed into the ultimate position of authority. He couldn't handle it. He left too much to his aides who he rarely if ever questioned.'

I couldn't help smiling at my friend's observations. The tone and the sentiment were heavily biased. His ideas were rather general within his department. He represented the view of the hard-core

95

British civil servant dealing with foreign affairs. Everyone was wrong, silly or incompetent – except their own people. His department specialized in Middle East affairs and had in its ranks a lot of former colonial police and army officers. Many of them had service going back to the old Palestine days and their contempt for Jews was only matched by their contempt for their own superiors. The Israelis were never referred to in the department, except in reports, as anything other than 'the Shonks'. The department leaned strongly, if irrationally, to the Arab cause in a way that sometimes made you think they were still dreaming of the days of T.E. Lawrence and the old Arab Bureau. In my dealings with the department I was always careful to play up to this biased viewpoint. The sentiments did not bother me overmuch. I was dealing in information. It precluded sentiment and emotion.

I had already packed a suitcase.

I left the Cumberland Hotel at 2.30, took a cab back to Chelsea, collected my bags and drove out to Heathrow to catch the 7 p.m. Pan Am flight to New York.

Eight hours later I checked into the Sheraton on Seventh Avenue, took a pill to work off the jet lag and at ten the next morning checked in to the *Penthouse* offices on Third Avenue.

The editor was an ex-*Life* magazine staffer, Ken Gouldthorpe. He was a Yorkshireman. Perhaps that is why I felt he was the only real newsman I ever met at *Penthouse*. He was fired after a row over editorial inefficiency long before the *Liberty* article appeared. Ken was a veteran of the 1960 Congo War. He was a reassuringly hard newsman of the old school. I was able to talk to him on common ground. His deputy, Peter Block the articles editor, was enthusiastic, determined and was picking up some of Ken's hardheadedness so I felt pretty confident so long as I had the two of them for back-up.

Gouldthorpe gave me an introduction to Bill Corson, the bureau chief in Washington, and I rented a car and travelled down late Friday to spend the weekend with some friends in Virginia. On Monday morning I drove into town and set up a meeting with Corson at the bureau offices on H Street.

Corson was a short, stocky ex-Marine colonel who had been in and out of political and military intelligence work all his life. He still maintained close and important contacts with the Washington intelligence community.

He was a very quiet, self-effacing man who worked without fuss and dug up information with an efficiency which must have made him a well-respected spy in his day.

I gave Corson the names of the contacts my Foreign Office friend had suggested and he confirmed they were good. He added some more of his own to the list and I began to make my calls. I decided to leave the official business I would need to conduct with the Navy PR people until I had got over the main inquiries; although Washington, like Beirut, is a place where you can inquire very little without everyone knowing about it within forty-eight hours.

The first good, positive contact was a State Department employee, who had a working knowledge of the Senate Foreign Relations Committee in 1967. He gave me a strong briefing on the initial reactions to the *Liberty* attack and the subsequent arguments which followed the internal controversy over it.

What he said in the main was that the Senate Foreign Relations Committee was in special session on the morning of the attack. Their reaction to the news was just as furious as the reaction of the military had been. But it was motivated by different reasons and directed against different culprits. No one told them the Israelis had attacked *Liberty*. 'It's the Russians,' Secretary of State Dean Rusk announced.

'They've escalated the war to direct confrontation,' Senator J. William Fulbright said.

How could they have been expected to intuit the truth? Even two days afterwards it was hard to believe, my State Department friend told me. A Pentagon spokesman was quoted as saying 'plausible explanation' could be found in human error. But immediately afterwards, Assistant Defence Secretary Phil Goulding rejected this, saying, 'We cannot accept an attack on a clearly marked non-combatant US naval ship in international waters "plausible" under any circumstances.' An admiral in Naval Communications made the comment that the attack had been 'another Pearl Harbor'.

Cries of outrage were also heard in the House of Representatives. Craig Hosmer, the Republican congressman from

California, called the attack 'high piracy' and demanded that the Israeli Government make full reparation to both the United States and the families of the dead and injured. He also said that open proceedings should be taken against the men responsible for the attack order and those who carried it out.

Congressman Thomas Abernethy, a Mississippi Democrat, criticized the government attitude. The Americans had taken the whole thing too lightly, he said, Washington was 'as quiet as the tomb' about the whole event. Where was American pride? Where was her indignation at this affront to her dignity?

Of course, Congressmen Abernethy and Hosmer, the Joint Chiefs, Goulding, and all the others who had criticized Israel's action had never been privy to the secret war plans of the CIA and the highest advisers of Lyndon Johnson. If they had been, they might have been appalled; but at least they would have understood the reluctance of the Government to approach the problem. Its plan was simple: it had to cool everything, to cover up.

According to one of the few leaks that came out of the secret congressional hearings on the *Liberty*, two of the pilots involved in the attack had been Americans – ex-Navy fliers. The story was not unlikely, because the Israelis had employed, and still do employ, trained American military personnel who 'emigrate' to Israel. A friend of mine now in the Dubai air police who patrol the Gulf, told me that just before he had taken the job in October 1973, the Israelis offered him a contract to fly as a helicopter pilot. He had been a trained Cobra gunship jockey in Vietnam. Although he never said precisely how much he had been offered, he was being paid in excess of $60,000 a year, tax-free, in the Gulf. He admitted that this was only slightly better than the Israeli pay. Also, while I was in Damascus during the Yom Kippur War, the Syrians produced some captured Israeli pilots for the Press. Two of them were Americans.

My story was now improving, really growing into something good. The possibility that Americans had flown against the *Liberty* certainly made the affair a whole lot more sinister. But I realized I didn't have to search for possibilities; there were now more than enough facts to confirm the early suspicions of Tito Howard. A wall of silence masked a complex scandal. The US Government had connived with the Israelis to hush things up. A clear-cut conspiracy had taken place.

Because every covert inquiry made in Washington in late 1975 was coloured by Watergate paranoia, each piece of dubious administration policy uncovered was always introduced by my informants as 'another cover-up'. The *Liberty* incident was one of many cover-ups by the Johnson administration. I began to think everything the US Government did was then followed by a 'cover-up'. When you told prominent people about a new cover-up scandal they just looked blank and said, 'Oh, yeah, right.'

With a strong pro-Israeli lobby in Congress and also in the Senate, there naturally had to be a counter-lobby. The anti-Jewish lobby in Washington was not nearly so strong but it included such men as Tom Ruffin, Richard Shadyak and Senator Him Abourezk of South Dakota. This lobby also had the support of some influential serving and retired members of administrations who, when presenting their views on the 1967 Middle East crisis, freely levelled blame at the men behind Lyndon Johnson. It was the Johnson advisers, the former Kennedy men they considered to be the bad influence who led the President to make a lot of dubious foreign-policy decisions. They ranked Johnson's Middle East policy alongside the decision to escalate the war in Vietnam. The man who urged Johnson along the Vietnam course was Walt Rostow.

Rostow's name had occurred continuously through my initial documentary research. He was a strange man. His quiet and studious appearance, balding and bespectacled, hid a hawkish soul full of the most warlike purpose. David Halberstam in his study of the Kennedy-Johnson administration, 'The Best and the Brightest', noted that one of Rostow's aides had described his chief's relationship with Johnson 'like Rasputin to a Tsar under siege'. There was nothing you could add about him that could be any more character-revealing or explicit.

Rostow was born in New York in 1916. He was one of three sons of a Russian-Jewish immigrant. He was something of a child prodigy, the youngest to graduate from school, an unusually young graduate of Yale and a Rhodes scholar. He studied at Cambridge and published regularly. His books were always being reviewed in the *New York Times*. As a member of the staff of the Centre for

International Studies at MIT, he published a book in 1953 called 'The Dynamics of Soviet Society' which was financed as a propaganda exercise by the CIA. This book was issued in two versions, one (classified) for the CIA and government policy-makers, the other (unclassified) for the public. Rostow had agreed to publish the book because he was in total accord with American policy to blunt the Soviet menace. He was the sort of man Joe McCarthy would have been proud to own.

In the late 1950s John F. Kennedy began to put together his famous intellectual think tank. It included Walt Rostow. He was well liked for his openness, his energy and his realistic approach to Washington politicians. He also got along well with the military and understood their viewpoints, unlike most Jewish intellectuals.

Rostow entered the Kennedy administration when the Democrats moved into the White House in 1960. Although John F. Kennedy played heavily on his liberal image, Rostow was allowed to continue pushing his hawkish anti-Communist theme in all foreign and domestic security issues. The day Che Guevara was killed, according to Halberstam Rostow reported to his staff: 'The Bolivians have executed Che. They finally got the S O B. The last of the romantic guerillas.' During his time with Johnson, pushing for the escalation of the Vietnam War he was reputed to have run through the corridors of the White House waving the daily reports of Viet Cong body counts and yelling 'they're going up and up, we're killing more of the bastards every day'. His attitude to Middle East affairs was very similar. Although he responded properly and angrily to the Israeli attack on *Liberty* he had, prior to the opening of hostilities in the Six Day War, been strongly in favour of helping Israel 'put the Communist/Arab menace in its place' – as reported in 'Nasser: The Cairo Papers' by Mohammed Heikal. Because of Rostow's reputation as perhaps the best of Kennedy's intellectuals, Johnson, certainly no intellectual himself, was overawed by the man's background and allowed him a virtually free hand in formulating and dictating American foreign policy where it related to national security. Rostow's was a dangerous policy: intellectually he was good but he lacked the slightest vestige of the true Democrat's sense of liberal fair play and anti-war fervour.

Walt Rostow was admittedly a hawk but he found his real vocation as an anti-Communist zealot promoting the war against North Vietnam. It was a policy totally in opposition to the declared opinion of American Jewry which argued strongly against the Vietnam War. The Six Day War helped change this sympathy. By taking a strong role in support of Israel against the Arabs, on Rostow's advice, Johnson turned many of the Jewish doves into hawks and gained their political and financial support for the war in Vietnam.

Writing in the *Wall Street Journal*, William F. Buckley observed: 'The Jews have been among the most dovish about the war in Vietnam. Administration men have almost maliciously enjoyed the way the Middle East crisis has dulled some of this Jewish dissent.'

Rostow now had a logical argument to offer as a reason for backing Israel. The administration needed Jewish support for Vietnam; Lyndon Johnson, like them or not, needed Jews, their votes and their cash. Rostow told him that if America was prepared to stick its neck out for Israel, for the Great Jewish Principle, then the Jews with their rational common-sense business instincts of excluding like for equal like, would support the war against Vietnam.

The $5\frac{3}{4}$ million Jews in the United States represent only three per cent of the population. There were only eighteen Jewish Senators and Congressmen. But the heaviest contributions to both the Democratic and Republican parties were from Jewish sources. In politics, as in everything else in America, money usually had the final say. It made the minority an effective vocal majority. When Rostow urged Johnson to back Israel the President could only say yes.

When I offered the idea of America wanting to push Israel against Nasser in a Suez-type operation I was told by the pro-Arab lobbyists that this was indeed true. It was a plot hatched by the US government, the big oil companies who were trying to recover ground lost to Arab nationalists, and the Israelis who were doing it in return for land. The man at the centre of the plot was Senator Jacob Javitts of New York. And of course there were Arthur Goldberg and the Rostows.

The pro-Jewish lobbyists had a similar hypothesis to offer, but without the suggestion of a Jewish plot. They argued that the American Government had tried to end the crisis by negotiating with Nasser; that Nasser had refused to negotiate and Russia had pushed the Egyptians into moving against Israel to prevent any possibility of a peaceful solution in that area from which both Israel and the West would have benefited.

Both versions were suspect. I decided they each probably carried a grain of truth, but at this stage it was difficult to assess its size and scope. I rejected the 'Zionist conspiracy' theory because it was far too banal to be part of an effort to reshape world politics. If it did play any part in the 1967 War, it was because the United States Government wanted to exploit the well-known Jewish fervour for the safety and preservation of the homeland for its own ends. The Americans were trying to counter the Soviets in an area (the eastern Mediterranean) where the Russians were determinedly building up their influence. The same thing has now happened in Africa but, lacking traditional ties or allies on that continent, the United States has been steadily losing ground to the Soviets. The day of the gunboat had gone, which the British Government learned to its cost at Suez in 1956 and the Americans were learning in Vietnam in 1976.

The great powers were like chess masters. They carried on their global strategic struggles using their wards as ethnic pawns. In the Middle East, American strength lay in its Israeli allies: it could go on the offensive against Russia only through them. The same in reverse was not true for Russia: the Arabs were neither prepared nor able to take the offensive.

Interviews with some ex-naval intelligence men, some strategic studies officers at the Pentagon and the CIA contacts my London friend had given confirmed that in the build-up to the '67 War the Johnson administration, the Pentagon and the NSA were in a flustered daze of fears about Soviet plots. Primarily, they were afraid the Russians were suddenly about to increase their naval presence and strike ability in the eastern Mediterranean in direct opposition to the US Sixth Fleet. This did not offer a direct confrontation challenge to NATO, nor was there any suggestion of a Soviet-inspired plan to agitate the Arab-Israeli confrontation. There was just an overall sense of paranoia about Russia which had lingered on since the end of the immediate post-1945 'Cold War'. Détente was a word nobody, probably not even Henry Kissinger, really believed in. The initial reaction of the Senate Foreign Relations Committee to the 'Russian attack against the *Liberty*' rumour was supplemented by the contention that the Soviets had hit the ship with 'carrier-borne jets'. Détente had done little to kill long-held suspicions of the treacherous Reds. The NSA had also warned Commander McGonagle that the Russians were increasing their Mediterranean naval presence with the *Moskva*, a 15,000-ton helicopter cruiser which was alleged to be carrying 'a wing of Yaks' and SA-N3 'Goblet' surface-to-air missiles. The Yakolev 36, NATO codename 'Freehand', is a Soviet V/STOL aircraft, a jump jet, which did not actually come into general service until it appeared with the Black Sea Fleet in 1976. The *Moskva* did travel from the Black Sea to the Mediterranean escorted by two destroyers, but did not arrive until 20 September, three months after the Six Day War was over. She was rumoured to be carrying thirty V/STOL jets. In anticipating the presence of a Soviet aircraft carrier prior to and during the Six Day War, either American intelligence was appallingly inefficient or the reports had been circulated purposely to create a greater sensation and add to the growing general alarm. The day the *Liberty* received the report the Sixth Fleet was placed on Def Con Four (Defence Condition Four) which is one alarm condition of combat above normal readiness. (Def Con One would be an order to launch a full-scale nuclear attack against Russia.) The Sixth Fleet and US armed forces in Europe were put on Def Con Three, again during the 1973 Arab-Israeli war. The order to go onto Def Con Four in June 1967 was not a major drama, but it did suggest that while accepting Russia was not about to escalate the confrontation situation the Pentagon were still treating them with caution and suspicion.

According to Pentagon, State Department and White House sources, US forces were not placed on Def Con Three in 1967 because a link established between President Johnson and the Kremlin reassured the American Administration that there would be no Russian participation in the war, so long as it did not extend beyond normal conventional methods. But the rumour concerning

Moskva put this reassurance in enough doubt to re-grade combat alertness from five to four.

At meetings held during the week before the war began between Department of Defence officials and the Military Attaché's Department of the Russian Embassy in Washington, the Soviet officials made it clear they did not wish to escalate the confrontation by active participation. Nor did they wish to insist on a joint American-Soviet front to clear up the Tiran Straits affair. However, they were insisting the United States give some categorical assurance that the conflict would not develop into full-scale war involving the bombardment of civilian targets and even into a nuclear-stage war in the unlikely event of the Arabs overwhelming the Israeli Army.

Israel had its nuclear reactor plant at Dimona and a number of missile sites in the Negev Desert. It was important that these be kept dormant and inoperative.

Johnson agreed to give this categorical reassurance. Because of it he was able to ring Soviet Premier Leonid Brezhnev on the hotline immediately he was informed of the attack on the *Liberty* and secure permission from the Soviets as guarantors of Egyptian air space for two wings of US Skyhawk and Corsair interceptors to enter Egyptian territory and cross the Suez Canal on the fastest route from the Sixth Fleet to *Liberty*'s position off Al Arish. Just exactly how Johnson was able to guarantee the Israelis would not use nuclear missiles, despite the existence of a supposed 'Doomsday Plan' to launch a nuclear attack on Arab cities if Israel was about to suffer defeat at the hands of their enemies, no one would tell me. I was told that the CIA had drawn up a lengthy report on the Israeli 'Doomsday Plan' and this contained detailed contingencies to prevent its application. I was told only that definite guarantees had been made. President Johnson had been assured by the Joint Chiefs of Staff and the NSA chiefs including Richard Helms, Director General of the CIA, that it would be possible to 'negate the Israeli nuclear capability'. The whole matter of Israel's progress in the nuclear field had been deliberately withheld from the US Government, even from the CIA, by the Israelis – though the Americans believed differently. Perhaps James Angleton and his close associates at counter intelligence knew exactly where the

Israelis stood in strength and intention with their nuclear weapons. But at every other level Israel was prepared to keep its plans and its contingencies to itself. It had to remain the lone wolf to prevent outside interference.

When the war actually started the United States immediately discovered it had been a victim of a counter intelligence plan brilliantly conceived by General Dayan and his civilian and military intelligence chiefs. By withholding news from the battlefronts and putting a total censorship ban on the early announcement of Israeli victories, Dayan hoped to befuddle both friends and enemies alike and keep them from retarding his advancing troops. Documents made available in 1977 under the Freedom of Information Act and from my own State Department sources confirmed that Dayan personally gave the order to attack and sink *Liberty* to prevent the ship breaking down his barrier of confusion and military secrecy.

I reasoned that evidence already proven and accepted about Dayan moving his forces under the cover of an information blackout provided a very credible reason why the Israelis should have attacked *Liberty*. Some experts in strategic studies argued that in terms of pure military logic, Dayan was right to order the attack. Morally it may have been a treacherous act, but militarily it was a daring stroke.

When I suggested this to some of the navy and marine officers I was dealing with, they told me I was trying too hard to be fair. One of them said to me: 'You only want to write that so the Israelis will think you're not such a bad guy after all. It's a typical liberal idea. You're everyone's neutral friend.'

I thought about this soon afterwards and again many times while writing the *Penthouse* article and this book, and decided I could see the strategic reasons behind Dayan's attack but I couldn't agree with them myself.

When talking to my military contacts I kept sentiment apart. Soldiers take defeat hard and even eight years after *Liberty* the US Navy was still smarting and hell bent on revenge which they called 'putting the record straight'. You could never get the Navy to look at the killing of thirty-four sailors on a virtually defenceless ship, in the same way as commanders at the Institute for Strategic Studies did: as a technically 'interesting' situation.

The CIA felt just about the same way as the Navy.

Before the war the US Government's military agencies had been involved in what they thought a profitable alliance with the Israelis. Within two days of the war starting they realized any such understanding about just what the Israeli Army should and should not do with regard to capturing and holding territory was null and void. At the negotiations in January and March and on 24 May, immediately prior to the onset of war, the Israelis had promised to limit their objectives to simply inflicting the necessary humiliating defeat on Egypt to put an end to the Nasser régime. If King Hussein got involved in the fighting, then any Jordanian territory captured would be held strictly for a temporary period during the combat. There was to be no occupation of the West Bank or the Old City of Jerusalem. The CIA knew these were prime targets. They were not just political targets; they were also historical and religious. They represented an achievement of conquest only Jews and Muslims could understand. The religious principles of the people of Judaea were lost on the planners at the CIA. They were interested in US–anti Soviet strategy and politics. So the Israelis made no pleas and asked for no understanding of their purely Jewish case. They plotted along with the Agency. They agreed with every American principle to destroy the Soviet presence in the Middle East. They even conceded the need for a new 'western understanding' with the Arabs to protect the oil supplies.

But on 5 June they launched their plan. Their strategy was written by their own leaders. By 10 June they had achieved all their objectives despite America. If it was true, as rumoured, that Moshe Dayan had been the head of strategic planning, he had effectively and single-handedly played the CIA at their own game and beaten them. The Agency were not pleased, but there was nothing they could do about it. The attack on *Liberty* precluded any chance America would have had of exposing the Israeli dupe. To openly admit the ship's mission would have drawn severe political censure on the Johnson administration. It would also have been a severe military setback for both America and NATO in anti-Soviet operations in the Middle East. Neither the President nor the Pentagon wished to expose themselves and their covert operations to the public scrutiny of world opinion. This was exactly the situation Russia needed to force a whole new set of issues over Vietnam. It would have proved to be the Middle East's 'US Incident'.

When Moshe Dayan was first faced with the outrage of the Pentagon over *Liberty*, he told them if they exposed the true mission of the ship he would in turn expose the extent of American covert anti-Soviet operations against Egypt, Syria and Iraq. The Pentagon backed off. The US Government called an almost immediate closure to the file on the incident and made concessions to the Israelis so subservient and startling that they were hard for the professionals in the State Department and the senior officers in the Pentagon to believe and almost impossible for them to accept although, in the end, they had to give their acceptance. They have never stopped saying how reluctantly they gave it.

One of the most outrageous aspects of this cover-up so far as the Navy was concerned was the way in which the commendations for the ship's and McGonagle's Medal of Honour were submitted to the Israelis for approval. According to a member of the State Foreign Relations Committee's staff at the time, the citations were censored by Israel before they were awarded. All reference to the nationality of the attackers was deleted and McGonagle's citation read simply that his ship had been attacked by 'jet aircraft and motor torpedo boats'. The citation awarded to the ship referred only to 'foreign jet fighter aircraft and motor torpedo boats'. By allowing the citations to be censored the American Government condoned the attack on *Liberty* by conspiring with the attackers to cover up their identity.

On 11 June, 1968, Commander, now Captain, William McGonagle received his Congressional Medal of Honour at the Washington Navy Yard at a full-dress ceremony presided over by Secretary of the Navy Paul Robert Ignatius. That was the final formal public reference to the USS *Liberty* by the military. And still never a mention of Israel's part in her death and destruction.

In May 1968 the Israeli Government paid $3·3 million to the families of the thirty-four *Liberty* dead and one year later paid a further $3·5 million to the 171 wounded.

The US Government claimed $7 million compensation for the ship. The Israeli Government told them firmly they were not going to pay it, so what were the Americans going to do about it?

I asked the State Department officially what the position was at

November 1975 over the outstanding $7 million. They said it was still outstanding and still being processed. It was going through 'diplomatic channels'. 'After eight years?' I said. 'It's still going through diplomatic channels after eight years?'

'Yes,' the State Department press spokesman said dully. 'That's what I'm told. I just pass on what I'm told.'

When I reported this conversation to a senator friend of Bill Corson's he laughed and told me that not only had the Israelis not paid the damage claim on the ship, they hadn't paid the personal claims either. These were paid directly by the US Government as if they had been monies from the Israeli Government to preclude any embarrassment and threatened private law suits by the relatives of the dead and injured. Not a cent was deducted from Israel's Foreign Aid handout. At the same time the quota of arms shipments to Israel was increased. One member of the Joint Chiefs of Staff noted the Israelis were getting more US weapons, 'maybe to use against more US servicemen'.

I put this to an Israeli press spokesman. It was, he said, a complete lie, Israel had paid gladly to atone for its awful mistake. Which is precisely what I had expected him to say.

On 16 November 1967 a foreign-aid bill being passed through Congress included nearly $5 million for various Israeli educational programmes. Congressman Harold Royce Gross of Iowa demanded to know why the US Government was handing out multi-million-dollar grants to the Israelis when there had still been no reparation for the *Liberty* incident. He proposed an amendment to the bill providing that no funds would be paid to Israel in the Foreign Aid Programme until the Israelis had made satisfactory compensation to both the US Government and the families of the *Liberty* dead and wounded. The amendment was defeated.

Chapter Nine

The *Liberty* story now contained two issues for me to study and investigate.

The first issue was the background to the ship's mission which resulted in the attack. This background contained the American/Israeli deal before the war, the paranoia of US anti-Soviet policy in the Middle East and the strange counter-action of the Russians which was intended to push Nasser into a confrontation situation. These were all ingredients of a typical Russo-American politico-military crisis of the period.

The second issue was the post-*Liberty* crisis. This was principally a political cover-up of the State Department–Pentagon CIA foul-up over the pre-planning which led to the Six Day War. But on a more personal level it was an issue over compensation.

The *Liberty* families were caught in the middle. They were the ones raising their voices demanding to know why the ship had been hit, why the US Government had done nothing about it and why they were not being more adequately compensated for the death and the maiming of fathers, sons and brothers.

Those were the first, basic issues they raised. Later, they also wanted to know why their simple requests for fair and compassionate treatment were being met with hostility; why they were being threatened with a variety of bureaucratic reprisals if they did not remain silent while it was being 'sorted out'.

All levels of the administration and the military were helpful in providing me with even the most intimate details of the attack and the bravery of the ship and its crew. It was when I started to inquire about the harassment of claimants for compensation and the non-payment of compensation monies due that I met a wall of silence.

I must have spoken to almost every secretary in the Administration. Their bosses never returned my calls.

So far I had barely advanced far enough on the compensation

issue to get sufficient hard facts to even start to nail down the State Department. I had plenty of theory on the attack background, some of it supported by documentation and reliable interviews, but most of it hearsay. Even so, it had enough substance to be promising. The compensation investigation was so far pretty empty.

The only really dubious character who had emerged from my investigations was the 1967 Israeli Deputy Ambassador to America, Ephraim Evron. Obviously there were going to be many more, but 'Eppy' Evron was notable for his previous form in Mossad 'dirty tricks' operations.

'Eppy' had always been a Mossad man but had undergone a severe setback in 1954 when he organized the attempted bombing of the US Consulate in Cairo to stir up anti-American feeling. His cell of agents were grabbed by the Egyptian Secret Police and put on an elaborate show trial. Nine of them were captured. Two were executed and the others were given long prison sentences. His immediate chief at that time was Defence Minister Pinhas Lavon who was heaped with blame by Premier David Ben Gurion and made to take all the responsibility for the failure of the operation. He was totally disgraced. The affair went down as a black mark in Israeli military history. It has always been referred to since as 'the unfortunate affair'. But despite its scandal and notoriety it failed to record the other principals of the Ministry of Defence in the affair, 'Eppy' Evron and Moshe Dayan.

In 1967 they were together again in another dubious affair to promote Israeli interests at the expense of her American ally. They flashed into the *Liberty* story almost like a friendly old double act. One felt it surely would have not been the same without them. They gave my investigations a new perspective. I would pursue it when I went, as I planned to do, to the Middle East in early 1976. Evron and Dayan were experienced professionals. They left only the faintest trail behind them. But it was enough. There was still the scent of Cairo, 1954, clinging to Israel's continuous plan to sabotage any closing of the gap in US–Arab relations. I was sure *Liberty* had played a prominent role in this conflict of ideas and ideals.

I decided it was time to capitalize on the introduction my London banker friend had promised me to Navy Secretary Bill

Mittendorf. I had a written note given to me before I left London and my contact had also written independently to Mittendorf, explaining I was working on a Navy story and that I wished to discuss it with him.

I left a message with his office giving a contact number in McClean, Virginia. That evening his secretary telephoned and made a luncheon appointment. The phone conversation was informal and from the things she said Mittendorf seemed enthusiastic for a meeting. The secretary gave me the numbers of various naval personnel in PR whom Mittendorf had instructed to assist me with my inquiries. When I spoke with them I explained my mission fully. They told me they would return my calls with the answers to my various questions. They never did.

Two days later, the day before my lunch with the Navy Secretary, his secretary telephoned to say the appointment would be impossible. She would not explain why. I was both disappointed and intrigued by the reaction. My London friend was close to Mittendorf and his recommendation carried weight. But obviously it was not enough, even though Mittendorf was a man with a strong reputation for courtesy and integrity. His refusal to see me was a mystery. When I discussed it later with my banker friend he said the Navy Secretary had almost certainly been instructed from a higher place not to meet me, once the people in the Administration could see the trail my inquiries were taking. Mittendorf had been warned off. I returned to London from Washington and hung around the apartment for a week waiting for a return phone call from my Foreign Office contact who was away on a pre-posting leave before taking up a posting to Hong Kong in early January.

Tito Howard made another brief appearance in my life during that week, announcing that he was en route to Kuwait, Dubai, Riyadh and Baghdad. On my second day back the telephone calls from Hong Kong started again, with others from Sydney and Los Angeles. I assumed he was still in business in Australia. I gave Howard the basic background to my information-gathering trip to Washington, and he thought the stuff I had was 'dynamite'. It would really hurt the Zionists, he said. I asked him if he knew much about the compensation issue and he said he did. He had interviewed some *Liberty* survivors for his forthcoming documentary film on the incident (which is still forthcoming) and they told him shocking tales of threats by people from naval intelligence, from the CIA, from the State Department and even from the Internal Revenue Service. He was too involved with the Australian business to help me with the *Liberty* investigations, he said. He also told me that there would be no problem with continuing finances for my *Liberty* investigations, since Fischer intended to use the story I was piecing together to crucify Bob Hawke, the left-wing trade-union leader in Australia. Howard claimed that Hawke was a rabid Zionist who was trying to negate Whitlam's anti-Israel policies in the Third World.

'Good for you, Tito,' I said. It all sounded just a little bit tricky and involved.

Tito Howard left for Fulham. I went through the Australian notes I'd made and wondered if I should have kept on the trail of the story which seemed to be emerging there. On 11 November the Queen's representative, Sir John Kerr, had sacked Whitlam as Prime Minister, removed the Labour Party from government and replaced it, pending a general election, with the Conservative Malcolm Fraser as caretaker Prime Minister. From snips of Tito Howard's conversation on the matter, he and Harry Fischer appeared to have more than just a passing interest in it. But how much more I did not know.

Tito took off the following night for Baghdad. Before leaving for the airport he advised me to ditch Guccione and *Penthouse*, and leave him to fix a *Liberty* deal. Rupert Murdoch would buy the story for $20,000, he said. It sounded fantastic, only *Liberty* was not worth $20,000 at that stage and certainly not to Rupert Murdoch. Why should he suddenly appear in the affair, anyway?

The Australian newspaper proprietor had been nicknamed 'the dirty digger' by the satirical magazine *Private Eye* because of the penchant for scandal of his two principal London mass-circulation papers, the daily *Sun* and the Sunday *News of the World* which specialized in searching out and publishing banal and sensational stories either wholly composed of or liberally laced with sex. I did not see the dirty digger as a political animal, taking a stand for the rights of a couple of hundred Americans who had been shot up eight years before because their government had made a nonsense

112

of its devious foreign-policy planning. But I could see Murdoch wanting to sabotage Bob Hawke, Zionist or not, because of Hawke's association with Gough Whitlam and his stand for the Australian trade unions, which Murdoch despised and hated.

The prospect of getting $20,000 was tempting, but I had promised to forget the Australian affair in return for help on *Liberty* from the Foreign Office people, so I had to push it aside.

I repacked my canvas suitbag on 15 December and drove back to Number Three Terminal at Heathrow and took off for Nairobi. My friend from the Foreign Office had answered my call that morning.

'I made arrangements for you to talk to Major McKenna, the chap I told you about from the Gulf. He is staying at the Muthaiga Club until January the 5th.'

It had been two years since my last visit to Kenya.

Nairobi was constantly changing but I could still recognize it as the place where I found my first job in the spring of 1958. It did not seem so long ago although a great deal had happened during the last seventeen years.

I arrived at Embakasi at 8 a.m. and rang my brother's home. There was no reply. I rang his office at Police HQ, and I was told by the second-in-command of the Presidential Escort Section he was in Europe on business.

I rented a car and took the ring road round to Muthaiga, cutting out the rush-hour Nairobi traffic.

The Muthaiga Club was as it had always been. The stuffed lion was still there in the entrance lobby. When Britain officially left East Africa the last remnants of the colonial empire withdrew into retirement at the Muthaiga Club.

I asked the head porter if a Mr McKenna was living in.

'Yes, Mr Pearson. Major McKenna arrived a week ago. He's in the breakfast room. Would you like me to take you through?'

He led me ceremoniously through a cluster of tables, most of them occupied by single men with their heads buried in the *Standard* or the *Daily Nation*.

A man of about my own age was sitting near the french windows which were open on to the lawns. He was wearing a dark blue cotton shirt with a yellow on red polka-dot silk scarf inside the open collar. Over the shirt he wore a sleeveless bleach-washed khaki bush jacket. He had on long khaki trousers, bleach-washed to the colour of his jacket, and brown suede desert boots tinted slightly red by the impregnation of sand and murram dust.

'Excuse me, Major,' Joseph said. 'Mr Pearson has arrived.'

McKenna looked up from his copy of the previous day's London airmail edition *Times*. His eyes were the washed-out blue of a man who has spent his life in hot climates.

'Sit down. Anthony, isn't it? Or do you prefer Tony?'

'Tony. I believe you've just come down from the Gulf?'

'That's right, old boy. But really it's just as well not to talk too much about it. We are supposed to keep a low profile.'

The coffee arrived. 'How long are you staying?' McKenna asked me.

'A week. I'm down the road at my brother's house in Karura Avenue.'

'Ah. You're the brother of the President's bodyguard Commander? Now, tell me exactly how you need my help. Brian asked me to chat to you about the Six Day War, but I'm afraid my involvement in it was only a very modest temporary attachment to our people in Cyprus and Tel Aviv. Anyway, let's not discuss it now. Old Brian in London tells me you know quite a bit about the fishing here. I was wondering if I could tempt you to a couple of days up in the Aberdares? The warden is a friend of mine.'

'OK. That sounds good.'

'Capital. We can chat over our business at the Outspan at the weekend.'

The lawns of the Outspan Hotel at Nyeri in the Kenya Highlands look out across the forest to the peak of Mount Kenya. There, for two full afternoons, McKenna talked about his mission in the '67 War. He told me how he had discovered the build-up to the war while working undercover in Yemen, how he had been posted first to Cyprus then to Israel, and how he had been assigned to study the *Liberty* incident, following up his work in Israel.

'Why exactly was that necessary?' I asked.

'Because *Liberty* was monitoring stuff along the same lines I had been ordered to study, so my superiors decided I should have a chat with a couple of her officers.'

'Can you remember their names?'

114

'Sorry, old boy. Wouldn't tell you if I could. The chats I had were all off the record and confidential. What I can tell you is that the background you've pieced together so far is accurate. The American Government – not just the CIA – was working on setting up a new foreign policy in the Middle East to recover the ground they were losing to Russia. To do this, they had first to remove the initial obstacle which was the popular political success of radical left-wing Arab nationalism, as exemplified by our old friend, the late Abdul Nasser. Basically the Egyptian Army is conservative and right wing, so it was reasonable enough for the Yanks to think that if they encouraged the Shonks to go to war and they duffed up Nasser badly, he would lose his popular glamour and be booted out of control. Egypt would return to its old pre-Nasser conservatism, the Sovs would get chucked out along with Nasser and the Yanks would move in.

'The thing went wrong because the Israelis didn't really care a hoot for the Americans' motives behind the plan. They wanted territory. And they got it by confusing everyone so much with their suppression of real war information and the release of phoney bulletins, that before the Yanks realized what had happened and were in a position to put a stop to it, your Jew had grabbed Sinai, the West Bank, Old Jerusalem and the Golan Heights. All they needed to put the cap on their total land objective would have been the Litani river area of South Lebanon.

'These invasions were far in excess of anything the Yanks wanted. The American idea was that the Israelis should trounce the Gyppo army, even push them to the bank of the Canal, but should then retreat to a defensive line at the Mitla and Gidda Passes. The Americans on no account wanted an Israeli occupation of the East Bank of the Suez because of the effect it would have on the Canal, although they were glad enough that the Jews did set up the Bar Lev Line after Nasser hung on with his Russian backers. Even if Suez was closed to western sea traffic, it was also closed to the Soviets. But when the Jews made their first grab at the Canal, the Yanks weren't so pleased. Before the war started it was made clear to the Israelis that King Hussein had to be handled with kid gloves. He was the only real friend America had in the Arab world, along with King Feisal, and they calculated that if Israel made any

115

intrusions into Jordan territory it would alienate Feisal as well as Hussein. The United States could not afford the risk this would create to their oil supplies. Feisal had always insisted in his dealings with the West that Jordanian sovereignty must be assured, that Arabs' rights to Old Jerusalem must be guaranteed and that there would never be Israeli expansion into Syria and Lebanon.

'The whole thing fell apart at the seams when Israel attacked Jordan. Hussein had entered into an alliance with Nasser only a few days before the war started, to keep solidarity in the Arab world. Nasser was beginning to get wind that the CIA were after him and was saying in public that his enemies were plotting with the Americans and their Zionist friends. He actually had no proof of this at all, other than hearsay passed on by the KGB. By going to Cairo, pledging support to the Arab cause and promising his endorsement of Nasser's great plans for Arab unity, Hussein did a lot to clear away the slurs his critics had levelled against him.

'When the war started he naturally mobilized his army in a show of Arab strength, but only in a defensive role because he knew quite well he had no chance of adopting a belligerent posture.

'Launching their attack against Jordan the Israelis hid behind the faith Hussein had in American guarantees and promises of support. When the time came and the Israelis hit Jordan, Hussein and his forces were totally unprepared for the devastation heaped on them. By never publicly censuring Israel, which it could have done by giving out the full details of its promises to Jordan, the Johnson Administration connived at the whole bloody deceit.'

McKenna paused and took a long pull at his drink.

'I can see you're leading to a point I think I already understand. It's about how the *Liberty* monitored the movement of Israeli troops against Jordan in contravention of the American agreement and started sending the stuff back to Washington so people there could pressure the Jews to withdraw before they completely cut up poor old Hussein?'

'Absolutely right. The Israelis were buggering about with the communications between Egypt and Jordan both by blocking them and by rewriting the reports to give both Arab armies a completely distorted picture of the way the war was going. In this way they were able to destroy resistance from Egypt and Jordan with

116

minimum loss to themselves and do it in the shortest possible time. The time factor was vital because if the fighting had dragged on, the United Nations, backed by strong American representation, would have enforced a ceasefire and blocked any further incursions into Arab territory by Israel.'

'Wasn't there anything the Yanks could do to reverse the situation, along the lines of the action Eisenhower took in 1956?'

'Don't ask me, old man. I'm a soldier, not a politician. But in a nutshell I would say no. The Israelis had the US Government bang to rights. The Americans were reaping the rewards of dealing with the Jews in matters of covert policy.

'There is another aspect to the problem which may also provide you with a second idea as to why the *Liberty* was hit. This had to do with the missile complexes in the Negev Desert and the nuclear reactor site at Dimona, near Beersheba.

'While I was in Israel in 1967, I was given a special brief to examine the situation around Dimona and other selected sites close to it, and sites in the Negev, north-east of Eilat where Israel had missile complexes. These complexes were built mainly for Hawks, which had been supplied to Israel by America but with only conventional warheads. By 1967 the Israelis had enough plutonium to build a dozen or more atom bombs, and they had had the biggest and best arsenal of nuclear warheads in the Middle East. The Russians were not nearly so stupid as to give the Arabs nuclear-missile warheads. The US Government knew the Israelis had a nuclear capability but they did not understand its potential. They had sent U2 reconnaissance planes over the Negev, and they had photographed what looked like a range of fourteen missile sites north of Eilat. By May these had increased to twenty sites. At this stage, the CIA started to wonder if the Israelis were not being quite honest with them.

'I made a close study of the Negev Desert area and the area around Dimona and concluded the Israelis had greatly reinforced their missile batteries on or just before May the 28th, barely more than a week in advance of their strike against Egypt.

'When I spoke to my opposite number in US military intelligence at the American Embassy in Beirut, he told me all his pre-war briefings made absolutely no reference to Israeli missiles and he

117

believed this was a deliberate omission. But my boss in Tel Aviv during the war said we particularly had to watch the Negev because the Americans had assured the Russians that if Israel tried to escalate the fighting to include ICBMs, then they would personally intervene to suppress the action of their wards.'

'Just how would they do that?'

'Do you know about the *Andrew Jackson*?'

At this stage I didn't and it wasn't a piece of information I could bluff my way through.

'No,' I said, 'except that it was a Polaris submarine.'

'Right. It was assigned to work as a liaison with *Liberty*.'

'Why?'

'Can't tell you right now. But think about it. Try to get some facts about it, and then maybe I can help you pull it together.'

'Did the sub have something to do with the Israeli ICBM complexes?'

'I can't and won't tell you, except to say I think investigating the *Jackson*'s brief could be a valuable part of your story. Quite honestly, I only know about the matter as second-hand information anyway, but I will tell you that if you make the right sort of inquiries you will find the movement of the submarine quite easy to follow. It was working out of Rota, Spain, during its attachment to the Sixth Fleet, in exactly the same circumstances as *Liberty*. Although I am no longer a serving British Army Officer, the work I did in 1967 on behalf of my government and to some extent for NATO and the Security Council is wholly classified. I will help you along with stuff that is within public access but I can't discuss matters which were and still are totally classified. I should talk to the highest navy authorities you can on the USS *Andrew Jackson*, because they're the chaps who are most likely to give you material, first because it's their problem, and second, they must be the ones to decide if it is to their advantage or not to talk to you. Some of the senior Pentagon men may well feel that continuing to keep the full story of their intelligence operations in the '67 War under wraps is more like a nasty conspiracy of silence than a strategic classification of vital military information which could be used to advantage by the enemy. Frankly, everyone concerned knows that the Russians are fully conversant with the whole operation from start to finish. NATO has ample evidence of similar Russian activities. You now have a situation of what the Americans call a Mexican stand-off. You will find most classified military material remains classified to keep up this condition of balanced blackmail, one side trading its silence for the other side's silence. To some extent I'm caught up in it too.'

He took his pipe from the side pocket of his bush jacket and filled it slowly with rough shag from his leather tobacco pouch.

'In 1967 I changed all my ideas,' he said. 'When that war started I was all for the Shonks – you know, God's clean people and all that and how they were Europeans against the rest. But I don't believe it any more. I don't believe in South Africa either any more. I feel sorry for the chaps down in Rhodesia but I don't believe in them. Sometimes I wonder why I am working in the Gulf but I do try to believe that the status quo there is right and we must keep the worst sort of Commies away from the Arabs.' He paused.

'I hope the stuff on the ship is good enough for you. It's the best I can do. I get terribly conscientious in my old age, I'm afraid. Anyway, when you finally put it together we can meet up and talk about it and maybe I can help you cap it. But right now I would much rather drop it and talk about fishing.'

I flew from Nairobi to Cairo via Addis Ababa and was met at the airport by an officer from the Egyptian Ministry of Information.

As always, the Egyptians were hospitable, cheerful, full of enthusiasm for my project and totally unable to understand my impatient western demands to arrange short-notice interviews with people relevant to my research. After spending five days sitting helplessly in the Nile Hilton waiting for appointments which never materialized and listening to people at the Information and Defence ministries constantly telling me to be patient, which I am not, I phoned General Shazli, the Egyptian Ambassador in London, and asked for his help. Immediately, things began to happen.

I received a call from a friend of Shazli, a man in the Ministry of Foreign Affairs who had been a high-ranking intelligence officer during the Six Day War.

He confirmed everything I already knew and told me that the first Egyptian reaction to *Liberty* was that she had taken up position off Gaza to spy on Egyptian-Russian radar and missile installations. However, he later heard that the ship was really spying on Israeli missile installations and that after a public outburst by Nasser claiming that the presence of the USS *Liberty* constituted actual American involvement in the war on the side of Israel, President Johnson had spoken to Leonid Brezhnev on the White House–Kremlin hotline and told him that *Liberty* had been sent to the area 'to keep an eye on the Israelis' and that if Israel tried to use ICBMs with nuclear warheads, the US Navy had orders to 'negate' the Israeli missile complexes in the Negev Desert before they could be used.

This information had been recorded in KGB files which came to light in 1972, two years after Nasser died and was succeeded by Anwar Sadat.

In May 1972 Sami Sheraf, the head of the KGB in Egypt, was arrested with Vice-President Ali Sabry, Interior Minister Sharawi Gamaa and War Minister Mohommed Fawzi for plotting against the State. The arrests followed an attempted coup against Sadat. The culprits were tried and all sentenced to terms of imprisonment for life.

The trial exposed the extent of Soviet plotting against Egypt. It had started before the 1967 War when the Russians began to realize that their assessment of their influence in the Arab world was not nearly as good as they had first believed. They realized Nasser was using them for his own ends and for the policies he had drawn up for the advancement of Arab nationalism. He was not soft on Russia nor did he offer any ideological support of Communist principles.

In the light of these revelations Egyptian intelligence began to build up a much clearer picture of the real Russian involvement in the advancement of the Six Day War. Interrogation of Sheraf and his associates revealed that the KGB knew every minute detail of the American-Israeli plan to move against Egypt and depose Nasser. Instead of trying to counter it the Russians urged Sami Sheraf to continually pass on rumours to Nasser that the Israelis were about to make war on Syria and then, having defeated the Syrians and broken the alliance of the UAR, they would turn on Egypt. As proof of this, Sheraf pointed to the supposed movements of 'thirteen Israeli brigades' on the Golan Heights front and urged Nasser to mobilize his own forces as a feint to deter the Israelis from an attack against the Syrian Army.

The KGB logic in feeding Nasser these lies and inducing a general sense of alarm in the Arab world was to prevent the Egyptian President acting in a low key towards a mounting Israel crisis which may have allowed the United States to review their situation, abort their anti-Nasser plan and open a political initiative which would probably have resulted in a phasing-out of Russian involvement in Egypt and a phasing-in of American aid to replace it.

The Russian evaluation was that if Nasser was deposed they could install Ali Sabry in his place and improve their control and status in Egypt. At the war's end their evaluation proved just as wrong as the evaluation of American intelligence. No one outside the Arab world had realized how great the charisma of Abdul Gamal Nasser really was. He stayed on, until his death from a heart attack in September 1970, when he was followed by Anwar Sadat, the most virulent of opponents to Russia's intrusion in the Middle East. When Sheraf and the Ali Sabry group were arrested, tried and sentenced, the KGB retired, knowing that they had lost the game, for the time being at any rate.

I spent Christmas in Cairo and travelled into Israel over the Allenby Bridge on 28 December.

As the Israeli soldiers hurried me politely through the checkpoint past the lines of bawling Arabs with their heaped-up baggage and interminable ragged animals I was glad I was a European and that Israel had to accord me the privileges of one. It was a selfish pleasure, but I was tired.

I took the bus into Jerusalem. Despite a confirmed reservation the King David Hotel did not have a room. Fortunately there had been no confusion over my Avis car booking. I drove down to Tel Aviv and checked into the Plaza Hotel. I had lived there during the October War.

My first inclination was to telephone two good government contacts who lived just outside the city. But I decided to be careful. The telephones into the Plaza were almost certainly tapped. On 30 December I did lodge a formal request for information on the

Liberty with the military censor's office. The request was received politely and without apparent surprise or interest. All the officer I spoke to said was that there wasn't too much material and certainly there was nothing which had not already been covered. He would send what he had round to the hotel, he said.

It arrived next morning. I had a call to my room saying there was someone to see me in the lobby. She was a girl, about twenty, brown complexioned but with dye-streaked fair hair. She was in the attractive tan mini-skirted uniform of the IDF and had the insignia of a lieutenant. She had an open, pretty face and a wide, easy smile and manner. She handed me a package.

'I believe this is what you want, Mr Pearson,' she said. 'It is all there is available.'

I opened the package. It contained a summary of an Israeli Court of Inquiry held on 11 June 1967, which found the action by the IDF, 'beyond criticism and blame' and the behaviour of the USS *Liberty* 'suspicious and suspect'. The ship had invited attack by its furtive behaviour while under air surveillance and again when under attack by the MTBs. The report said that the captain of *Liberty* had 'shrouded the ship in smoke to cover his escape'. It did not mention that *Liberty* was burning and enveloped in smoke from the attack by Mirages. The rest of the Israeli case was contained in the papers: that *Liberty* was mistaken for *El Quseir*; that she was not flying an American flag and did not have US Navy identification marks. Also enclosed in the package was a full transcript of Micha Limor's statement to the press telling how, when the torpedo boats discovered they had made a mistake, an officer on the *Liberty* refused their offers of help and, cursing, told them to go away. The final document was a short account of the events leading to the Six Day War which amazingly still claimed that Israel only began fighting in response to Egyptian aggression and following a strike against them by the Egyptian Army.

I pointed this out to the lieutenant.

'Does your department still expect us to believe that you didn't start the war in '67?'

'Oh, don't worry about that,' she said. She laughed. 'The people there just hand out paper. They just try to give you as much background as possible to help your story.'

It was 11 a.m. The girl looked at her watch. 'Would you care for a drink right now?'

'Sure.'

'Why don't we go up to the Hilton? Do you know the Cocktail Bar there? By the way, my name's Ruthy.'

'Good idea.'

'It must be pretty dismal spending New Year's Eve away from home,' Ruthy said. 'Are you married?'

'No.'

'I suppose you're married to your work.'

'No. I take everything in its place.'

She laughed. 'I'm not married either, and I don't have a regular boyfriend right now. I guess maybe I will when I finish my service. There isn't really any point when you are doing army service. Why have one when you can have them all?' She laughed again. She was watching my reaction. Her eyes were bright and very pretty, very liquid. She had tinted the lids a light-blue shade and her long lashes were evenly painted with mascara.

'I think I remember you from the war,' she said. 'You were up on the Golan at Sasa, weren't you?'

I nodded.

'You are a friend of Nick Davies.'

So she knew Nick. That really was no surprise but it was useful to know when I got back to London. I could ring Nick at the *Daily Mirror* and check her out. 'That's right,' I said. 'I am a friend of Nick's.'

At the Hilton she ordered a Baccardi and Coke and I bought a cold beer. She was cool and careful and only dropped pertinent questions at exactly the right moment. She did not seem to be making an effort to find out what I already knew. She seemed more interested in the fact that I worked for *Penthouse* rather than my exact assignment for the magazine. She asked if I was also a photographer.

For the first and only time throughout my inquiries *Penthouse* was going to be useful. Ruthy's lifelong ambition was to be a photographic model. She knew *Penthouse* was a good place to start. And she was fiercely ambitious and had no objection to undressing and posing for a *Penthouse* photo set. I talked to her for a long time about it and convinced her I was in a good position to help. She was very excited about it. Her reaction and her ambition were most relevant to the success of my relationship with her. We could be of mutual assistance to each other.

We had lunch in the Hilton coffee shop which Ruthy paid for – 'It's on my PRO expenses,' she said. She stayed talking for a long time and it was after four when she went back to her office at Bet Socalov, having promised to call at the hotel for me later that evening.

Back in my room I lay on the bed and thought long and carefully about Ruthy. Common sense and my natural suspiciousness suggested she was assigned to watch me and to discover what important information I had and who had given it to me. On the other hand, she seemed eager to use me as a stepping-stone in her ambition to be a photographic model – but that could be a line too. Working for the military censor's office, she must have worked closely with plenty of influential photographers whose help could be enlisted with plenty of simpler favours than providing secret information. But it was the only good line I had. It just might help me if I could handle her right.

Ruthy phoned from the lobby at seven exactly. I put on a clean shirt and my denim suit and went downstairs. She was standing by the reception desk wearing a long, wine-coloured cotton dress cut low so her breasts showed nicely above the bodice. Her hair was brushed out long so it would look casual but she had worked on it with curling tongs to give it just enough sexy flounce.

We went to an Arab seafood restaurant at Jaffa for dinner and sat talking for a long time. I would like to be able to say for the sake of the drama and suspense of my story that she was a spy who planned to rifle my baggage, compromise me and then blackmail me into agreeing to burn my notes and forget my story. But she was just a girl. She was pretty and she was entertaining; and she seemed to believe I wanted to research and write the *Liberty* story honestly and impartially, and to do that I needed good information and close cooperation. Over the next few days we became close friends but she made no attempts, obvious or covert, to debrief me about information I had or about any of my contacts

124

inside or outside Israel. As a precaution I did rip all my Israeli contact numbers out of my pocket book and burn them. I felt badly about not quite trusting Ruthy. She tried hard to produce army, navy and air force contacts who could help. It was hard to find people connected with *Liberty*, she said. Nothing of any consequence seemed to be coming up until she phoned me on 4 January and told me she had found the pilot of a Phantom who was leaving Israel for the US and who knew one of the men who had flown the *Liberty* mission. We would have a meeting, Ruthy said, at the Hilton at 7.30 that night.

She was ten minutes late. The man with her told me he was born in Baltimore, Maryland, had served in the US Air Force as a fighter pilot in Vietnam and had gone to Israel to live with his parents in 1966 when he had been demobilized from the service. His parents had emigrated to Israel in 1959.

He joined the Israeli Air Force as a pilot-instructor shortly after he arrived in Tel Aviv. When the Six Day War broke out, he led a squadron of Dessault Mirages on a strike against Egyptian fighter-bases west of the Suez Canal. Between the war starting on 5 June and ending on 10 June he flew twenty-six missions including the strike on *Liberty*.

The attack was ordered by IDF general coordination control after the ship had been under surveillance for three days. He said he was told there was an enemy ship off Al Arish, that it was some sort of electronic spy ship and was probably Russian. The ship had been reported to be showing American markings and colours but a request had gone to the US Sixth Fleet for information on any of its ships in the area and a reply had come back by return saying the closest American vessel to the Gaza coast was 600 miles north-west. The pilot said he was shown the reports; one of his senior officers who liaised with military intelligence said he thought the ship must be some sort of joint Arab-Russian project, trying to disguise itself as a US Navy ship. The Russians alone would never do such a thing. The Arabs had to be involved in such an obvious and infantile attempt at concealment: it smacked strongly of the Egyptians. Three pilots flew the mission in three Mirages. One of the others was a Vietnam veteran and had served with the US Navy Air Corps. The other pilot was a native-born Israeli.

125

The US Navy markings were clearly visible before they hit the ship, and all three pilots asked for reconfirmation of attack orders before they made the first run.

Their specific orders were to aim for the antennae and radar tracking gear on top of the superstructure; and they did this coming in flat over the ship's stack and hitting their targets with rockets and cannon shells. On the second run they saw men dodging across the decks towards the forward and after machine guns so they made alternate runs, bow to stern and amidships, strafing the decks with their own wing-mounted machine guns to put down any attempt at return fire and to disable the ship for the MTBs they knew were on the way to deliver the coup de grâce.

The man from Baltimore said he could see exposed oil drums on the forward deck. He strafed these and dropped two sticks of incendiaries which ignited the oil drums and started a fierce blaze forward and amidships. 'The fires produced dense black smoke. At that stage the MTBs appeared in the area and the Mirages pulled back to base to let the IDF Navy finish off the attack.'

I asked him if the ship looked familiar, as an ex-US Navy Air Force flier. He said it certainly had the appearance of an American ship and was flying an American ensign. He and the other pilots twice asked for confirmation of their attack order and they were told the ship was not what it appeared and had definitely been identified by IDF intelligence as 'the enemy'.

'Did you see military service?' the pilot asked me.

'Yes,' I said.

'Would you have questioned orders after you had received double confirmation of them?'

'No,' I said. 'I would have done exactly what you did.'

'Thank you,' he said. 'With hindsight, I'm not proud of my action in the attack but I was only carrying out orders. My father was furious when we finally knew the ship was an American Navy ferret. He said, "The SS said they were only carrying out orders when they piled people into the gas chamber in Dachau." I told him it was different. "Not to talk nonsense," he said. But don't you agree it was different?'

I said that I did. I assured him I would have done the same

126

thing. 'Anyway,' I said, 'even if your people did know it was an American ship, maybe they had good reason to hit it. I'm not taking sides, I'm only trying to see it from your point of view.' I need not have bothered.

'There's no need,' he said. 'Ruthy told me about you and what you are doing, and I just wanted to set the record straight. I'm not trying to give explanations for the rights and wrongs of the attack. I am just telling you how it was for the pilots who did it. That's all.'

I finally left Tel Aviv for London on 9 February. I haven't seen Ruthy since, although she wrote to me after my original article appeared in *Penthouse* in May/June 1976.

I never did know whether she was just a public relations girl from the censor's office or a Mossad spy. She never placed any difficulties in my way and she never asked me any leading questions about my investigation. She helped me greatly by producing the pilot who, I had no doubt, was genuine.

I flew back to London via Paris. Tito Howard had written just before I left for Nairobi to say he would be passing through Paris on his way to a business meeting. I called the Intercontinental and was told Mr Howard had not checked in. On a hunch, I asked if Mr Harry Fischer was there.

'Mr Fischer checked out this morning.'

'I'm an associate of Mr Howard's. Could you tell me whether Mr Fischer has returned to Australia or gone on to the States?'

'I believe he's gone to the Middle East.'

'To Baghdad?'

'I'm afraid I don't know, sir.'

I checked into the Hotel Castille in the Rue Cambon and called a contact who worked for the Drug Enforcement Agency at the US Embassy in Paris.

'Look, Mike. I'm trying to get some information on a guy called Harry Fischer who is supposed to own some film post-production company called Sun Productions in the States. He's half French, and half Australian, and I should think the DST will have something on him.'

'OK, I'll check him out.'

Within the hour the telephone rang.

'It's Mike. Look here, good buddy, just forget about the Fischer guy. The DST don't have anything and wouldn't tell you if they did. Just cool the whole thing. It's a problem.'

'What sort of a problem?'

The phone was just buzzing. Mike had hung up. His tone had been very abrupt. He was either angry or worried or both. I didn't have time to explain that I wasn't writing about Fischer or investigating him for any serious reason. I had already promised the people in London I wouldn't touch the Australian thing. I was just curious. I also needed to talk to Tito Howard. It irritated me when people just hung up the phone without good reason or an explanation.

I made another call to an English friend, a retired Special Branch officer who lives in the 16th Arrondissement. I explained the problem. He was back on the line three hours later, suggesting we should meet at the Café de la Paix near the Opéra. He explained that the DST kept a permanent tap on his telephone line. He told me this every time I called him. I suppose it was for the benefit of the line-tap, just to let the DST know he was on to them. Otherwise his relationship with the French security service was excellent.

When we met, he began at once, speaking in a clipped, military accent.

'This chap, Fischer. Strange fish. He's been up to quite a bit with the PLO chaps on the Boulevard Haussmann and he's been seen coming out of the Libyan Embassy in the rue Keppler with this other chap, Howard. This chap Howard hangs around most of the Arab embassies. He seems pretty close to the Iraqis and the Kuwaitis. Fischer also has very good connections at the US Embassy. The DST tell me the Americans don't want him to be harassed or interfered with. The last few times he's been through here he has had no contact with the Americans. The DST say he is in business in Australia, America, the Middle East, and Europe and that his contacts here are all to do with his various business interests. Tito Howard has been working as an introduction agent to find new business in various Middle East countries. I believe they are selling the Iraqis frozen Australian meat and 40,000 tons of frozen chickens. That's what I'm told, old man . . . I am also told by London to remind you of your arrangement.'

'Thanks,' I said.

When I got back to Cheyne Place the next afternoon I expected to be deluged with messages. There was nothing in the mail box. I checked to see if there were any messages at the *Penthouse* office in Fulham. There were none, but Molly McKellar, the PR officer, told me to telephone before I left for New York and Bob Guccione would send his car and driver to collect me at Kennedy Airport.

I was glad to leave London. Currently there was no progress to be made on *Liberty* other than writing up my notes and tackling the compensation issue in greater depth. I rang my banker friend before leaving and asked if it would be any use trying to see Bill Mittendorf again. He said no, Mittendorf hadn't contacted him to discuss the matter but if he wanted to play it in low key, for whatever reason, then it was pointless pursuing the issue.

Chapter Ten

The weather in New York was freezing. It was so cold I could hardly breathe. After checking in at the Sheraton I went down the block to a deli and had a hot pastrami sandwich, two Miller's and a plate of cheese blintzes. I had been looking forward to this meal for a long time. The blintzes were particularly good. The last time I had eaten blintzes was with Ruthy in Tel Aviv, just before I flew back to London. The lost weeks were unreal. I had been to Africa, to Egypt, to Israel; had spent Christmas in Cairo and New Year in Tel Aviv; had travelled to Paris, becoming once more involved in an intrigue which spanned half the globe; had gone back to London, tired and depressed; and I was now in a Jewish deli on Seventh at 54th, eating cheese blintzes, watching the traffic passing down to Broadway and wondering how the hell I had got there.

The next morning I rented a car and drove down to Washington. I rang Bill Corson at the *Penthouse* bureau to see if there were any messages. He said there was one from a State Department contact and another from Mrs Toth, the mother of Stephen Toth, one of the dead *Liberty* officers.

I rang Mrs Toth immediately. She seemed anxious to speak to me.

'It's about time this thing was dragged out into the open,' she said. 'I'm sick and tired of the way we have all been treated. It was almost as if the whole thing was our fault. My husband Joe worked the best part of his life in naval intelligence and he knew what was going on. There are times when loyalty can be too much of a burden. Joe was loyal to the service, and he was proud when Stephen was commissioned and when he was attached to the intelligence section. But you have to be loyal to yourself and to your own blood kin. After Stephen was killed we wanted to know what had happened and how the Israelis were going to compensate the families of young men they had murdered in that most criminally reckless way. The navy intelligence people first asked us to keep quiet and when Joe insisted they started to get quite abusive. They said that as a retired naval captain and intelligence officer, Joe was required to keep trust in the matter and help the Navy hush it up. It was his responsibility to his dead son. Joe told them his only responsibility to his son was to find out exactly why he had been killed and what the government of Israel was going to do about it.'

For Captain Joe Toth, ex-US Navy retired, and his wife compensation was irrelevant. Nothing could repay or replace the loss of their son, which was why they understood they weren't the only ones involved. What about the families of Lieutenant Philip Armstrong and Lieutenant Jim Pierce who were neighbours of the Toths at Norfolk? Each of those dead officers had five children. That left ten children with two young widowed mothers living in navy accommodation and suddenly reduced to financial dependency on a naval pension.

'The Navy told us the State Department were dealing with compensation, and these State Department assessors came along and told my husband the compensation for *Liberty* victims was being assessed along the same lines as a train wreck in Ohio in 1959. Joe just exploded. He asked them how the hell could they compare the ruthless, cold-blooded murder of thirty-four American sailors on a virtually unarmed vessel with a damn train wreck in Ohio. The insurance assessors were very sullen and went away, telling Joe he would be "got in touch with".'

Mrs Toth was talking confidently and carefully, only pausing to check an occasional figure or a date. She was obviously pleased and anxious to finally pass on her tale which she said she had come to believe would never be exposed. She had written to the *Washington Post* with complaints about her harassment by government agencies before and after her husband's death in 1969. Nothing had been done about it.

She said that after their first visit to the State Department some men came back and told Captain Toth that, while no figures had yet been settled, they thought the compensation details they were drawing up would be 'adequate' and mentioned a sum of $9,000. They asked that a release form for that amount be signed. Captain Toth said although he considered that he and his wife could never be adequately compensated for the loss of their only son, the widows and children of Armstrong and Pierce should at very least be well provided for. The State Department told Captain Toth not to make trouble. The issue was a sensitive one. The captain told them to go to hell and, despite a serious heart condition, he set off on a series of trips between Virginia Beach and Washington to bring a suit against the State Department. He took legal counsel with a firm of Washington lawyers, King and King, where his old friend John McWater was a partner. The State Department told Captain Toth that he was a troublemaker. But he had some strong support in the Pentagon from another old friend, Admiral McCain, and also from Admiral Kidd, who had conducted the *Liberty* inquiry.

Captain Toth wanted to know what the Israelis were doing to censure those responsible for the attack if, as they said, it was an error. No one could tell him. The Israeli Ministry of Defence investigation had never gone beyond the bare statement that court martial of the culprits was being set up, and inquiries in Tel Aviv about it were practically fruitless.

A hard fight ensued. Reminiscing about it, John McWater said that the State Department was 'very difficult' and subjected both the lawyers and Captain Toth to 'harassment'. He declined to be specific.

Mrs Toth was more specific. 'They killed my husband,' she said. 'First my son, then my husband. The harassment took the form of threats and assertions that Joe was damaging national security and there was surveillance and pressure from people like the IRS. It was too much for his bad heart, it took a year to kill him, but it did. We got $40,000 finally, but it cost us half of that just chasing around. Joe was also claiming on behalf of the families of the other two officers and he got them $50,000 for each child; so each family got $250,000 tax free when the US Government finally made the Israelis pay up. I still don't believe it was enough. The compensation for the *Panay* was much more.' (On 12 December 1937, Japanese shore batteries and aircraft shelled the American naval ship *Panay* in the Yangtze River. Three men were killed and forty-three sailors and five civilian passengers were wounded. Within four months 'a large indemnity' was paid. It was said to be more than $10 million.)

In May 1968 the Israeli government paid $3·3 million to the families of the thirty-four *Liberty* dead. One year later they paid $3·5 million to the 171 who had been injured. The US Government had also supposedly claimed $7 million for the damage to the ship, but that claim slid away into the obscure mists of silence, along with the Israeli inquiry, the court martial, and the records of the confidential congressional hearings. To those few press inquiries still being made, the official explanation for the *Liberty*'s mission was that she had been conducting research for 'electromagnetic-propagation studies' and monitoring the evacuation of US citizens from war zones. The fuss over compensation had quietened down when the Toth claim was settled. None of the other families was prepared to discuss it. They seemed frightened and admitted that State Department officials had ordered them to say nothing. They signed release forms for the money they received, which was apportioned 'according to rank' and represented little more than regular veterans' benefits.

An organization had been formed in Linden, New Jersey, by Mr and Mrs Thomas Reilly, whose son Thomas Jr, aged twenty, suffered a fractured skull and had a piece of shrapnel lodged in his brain during the *Liberty* attack. The organization called itself the Committee for Immediate Action – Families and Friends of Victims of the USS *Liberty*. Its intention was to extract whatever money the members considered the Government of Israel owed them. The first positive move to force compensation payment was taken by Mr and Mrs Reilly, who lodged a suit against Israel for punitive damages of $50 million, accusing the Israelis of murdering and maiming innocent persons. The suit was lodged with the World Court at The Hague. A representative of the State Department visited the Reillys and asked them to withdraw the claim. They refused. They were told the US Government was representing both them and the relations of other victims. So what? they said. They still insisted on their own lawsuit. The court at The Hague ignored their request. It was subsequently suggested that it had done so following coercion by the US State Department. Because all things political are possible, it is significant enough that the Reillys were snubbed, nor were they the only ones.

Congressman Craig Hosmer also attempted to pursue the

Liberty mystery and its aftermath. On 18 October 1967, he told the House that he had written a letter to Dean Rusk twelve days earlier, asking for details of compensation payments. On the same day, 6 October, he had also written to the Secretary of Defence, Robert S. McNamara. Rusk, he said, had ignored him completely, and McNamara had replied in a cursory note that read: 'The matter is receiving attention and you will be advised further as soon as possible.' He never was. When I spoke to Hosmer about the matter in November 1975, he shied away from the questions, claimed he remembered the incident dimly, but did admit that his inquiries never got off the ground 'for one reason or another'. He would not specify what these reasons were. Then he hung up on me. Most inquiries ended that way.

After speaking to Mrs Toth I felt pretty confident that the rumours I had heard the previous autumn about the harassment of *Liberty* families seemed to be strongly based on fact.

I rang five more *Liberty* families and the response from each person was identical: alarm and fear. They all said, 'Please don't involve us. Please don't write about us.' They asked me to leave them alone and to forget about *Liberty*. I said it was important to reopen the inquiry. The compensation issue has never been satisfactorily solved. There were no records of the individual payments made other than those involving Captain Toth's lawyers.

I asked each individual I spoke to if they could give me some idea of the amount of compensation they had received so I could start to build up some sort of table to work out an average payment. No one would help. Mrs Toth was alone in wanting to re-open the case. She was the only one prepared to come forward herself and speak openly and freely. Her husband's lawyers, though polite, were not very helpful. They said the papers on the *Liberty* cases 'no longer existed'. They had been filed away and after the case was closed they were 'most probably destroyed'. One of my contacts on the Hill, a young man who worked in the office of a prominent senator, made some inquiries around the legal section of the State Department and found the Toth/Armstrong/ Pierce case notes had been requisitioned and either filed or destroyed, along with other *Liberty* papers, in September 1970.

On Tuesday, 12 September 1972, John R. Rarick, a Democratic

congressman from Louisiana with extreme right-wing opinions, brought up in the House the question of the still-unexplained attack on the *Liberty*; he demanded to know why it continued to be hushed up and why the families of the dead and injured had been treated so unfairly with regard to compensation. He got nowhere.

I spoke to him in November 1975 and he alleged the Israelis had never actually paid a penny. He said the money had been pushed through Foreign Aid as an extra. In effect the US Government had paid it. He also claimed that even as late as 1972 he was being harassed by the State Department and the security agencies for trying to stir up the whole business again. He said that nothing had been paid, other than regular benefits, and that claims for all punitive damages had been ignored except in special cases, such as Captain Toth's, in which there was a danger of dragging the US Government into the public courts.

'It's a double standard all the way round,' he said. 'The boys who survived will never discuss the money. It is as though they had been paid hush money or something. And of course there were the threats.'

I followed up my November talk with Rarick with another telephone inquiry to his home. I wanted to know more about the threats.

His response was very nervous. 'Leave me alone,' he said. 'I can't talk to you. Funny things happen to people who talk about the *Liberty* thing. I don't ever want to talk about it again. I can't talk to you. Please don't telephone again. I'm sorry.' He hung up. I tried him again. He hung up again. Then he wouldn't answer the phone.

That night I went to visit a friend in Falls Church, a former CIA employee. I had first met him many years ago in the Congo, just before Patrice Lumumba was assassinated. We were, therefore, through the vicissitudes of war, close friends, first in Africa and later in other places. He had been making his own inquiries for some weeks.

'There are still a lot of problems over *Liberty*,' he said. 'What exactly they are – and I mean what specifically and very precisely they are – I can't find out. That's the truth. You mention *Liberty* in the Agency, in the State Department, in the Pentagon – and you get a really weird response. Everyone acts either hostile or scared. One of the Agency people knows I'm friendly with you and told me I should be careful. He said *Liberty* was still "hot shit" in the Agency because of things surrounding the incident which so far have remained secret.

'It is a fact that there has been considerable harassment of anyone trying to raise the *Liberty* issue and if I were you I would tread carefully. I'm not trying to be dramatic. I just know what you're up against. So it's impossible to say exactly what you can expect. You really need some back-up. I suggest you go pay a call on Jack Anderson. He's raised *Liberty* a couple of times in his column. He seems pretty keen on the story and he's afraid of no one in this town, I promise you.'

I rang Captain McGonagle in Santa Barbara. I had been careful to avoid pressuring him. I knew he was bound to secrecy under various articles of the naval intelligence charter. When I spoke to him his voice was low and flat as if all the life and vitality had been drained away. Friends of his had told me that the combination of his serious wounds and the mental strain of the post-attack troubles had proved a severe mental and physical strain for him. He had tried hard to stand up and fight for his men but bureaucracy had beaten him, a hero holding the Congressional Medal of Honour, a man whom bullets, rockets, cannon shells, torpedoes and all the guile of the skilful Israeli war-machine could not beat. I felt disgust for a system that could push and hold down such a man. I said as much. 'I'm not trying to be difficult,' he answered. 'Maybe someday I can write my own book about it. Right now I can say nothing. You understand why?' I said that I did. But could I come to Santa Barbara to see him? 'No,' he said. It was better for him and for me that I didn't. He wished me every success. 'You're outside of it,' he said. 'Don't let them beat you. You're the last shot *Liberty*'s got left to fire.'

Before calling Anderson as my CIA friend suggested, I first called Robert McCluskey at the State Department, reminding him of our last meeting in Cairo during the 1973 War when Kissinger started jetting around the Middle East trying his 'shuttle diplomacy'. I had been most impressed by McCluskey's reputed talent as a Mr Fix-it. When Kissinger arrived at the Cairo Hilton, we saw a bevy of girls dressed in satin mini skirts and amply decorated with the most decadent of western make-up. Bob Southgate of ITN had commented on this sudden appearance of a commodity so far unseen during the October War but he added that the Yanks were famous for their ability to produce short and rationed commodities when no one else could find them.

Ray Coffey of the Chicago *Daily News* turned to us.

'You know,' he said, 'that Bob McCluskey acts just like he was Kissinger's trouble-shooter. Whenever there's a tough problem, Bob's the man. The thing to remember when you want a favour from Bob, is always to tell him no one else can do it. It appeals to his ego to achieve the difficult, or even better, the downright impossible.'

So now I was turning to McCluskey for a favour.

'Bob,' I said, 'no one has been able to give us an answer on the question I'm going to ask. They say it's downright impossible . . . '

McCluskey had been in charge of compensation payments in 1968 and 1969. To whom were they paid and what sort of figures were settled upon various individuals? Bob didn't remember. I pursued him for a week and then he turned up a man called Fabian Kwiatek, an assistant legal adviser in the International Claims Department of the Secretary of State's office. Mr Kwiatek's statement was as follows:

'One hundred per cent of them [*Liberty* families and survivors] agreed to accept the payment offered and the Israeli Government paid all the claims. All the hospital expenses were paid by the US Government. Altogether, sums of between $100 and $300,000 – no $200,000 – no, perhaps it was nearer $350,000 – no, more like $200,000-odd were paid.'

'That's very good, Mr Kwiatek. Do you have an exact record of what was paid to each claimant?'

'No. We don't keep those sort of records.'

'You mean to say the United States Government pays out almost four million dollars' compensation and does not record where it goes to?'

A long pause. 'Ah! Yes! I can't give you that information. It contravenes the intrusion-of-privacy bill.'

Soon afterwards I received a telephone call from an officer in the navy's Public Affairs bureau.

'We must meet for a drink,' he said. 'I've become really interested in this *Liberty* business. What really happened? I suppose you must know it all, and I would be really interested to hear what you have.'

'You'll be able to read it soon enough,' I said. That failed to amuse him. He didn't telephone again.

Finally, I had a last, uneventful talk with Captain McGonagle in California. Loyal to his military pledges, he was saying nothing. He sounded even more weary. He sounded like a man who had taken enough. Finished.

I called Jack Anderson and he immediately invited me to call on him in his office in Connecticut Avenue.

I told him that my problem was silence and hostility from various administration bodies. They either didn't want to talk about *Liberty* or else they tried to confuse me by giving me very patchy or totally misleading information.

'You won't believe how stupid these guys can be,' Anderson said. 'You know the Agency put surveillance on my house which was so obvious that my kid spotted them and took the car number. The number checked back to the Justice Department and they were so embarrassed at being spotted they confessed they had loaned the car to the CIA after a special request to do so to undercover the activities of the Agency men. You would think the Agency would be at least smart enough to use a car with plates which were at least not traceable back to the public service. But that's the trouble with the administration. Even its spies are so hyped by bureaucracy they have to fill in every requisition in triplicate and they're put outside a journalist's home in a car carrying plates tracing it right back to the Justice Department. I called them the next day and demanded they take the tap off my phone. I didn't know specifically that they had one on but I thought I'd throw the complaint in for good measure. They were really embarrassed and apologetic.

'Anyway,' Anderson said, 'to get back to your story. If I were you I would keep on plugging the compensation issue and demanding that the State Department tell you why the Israelis haven't paid up the $7 million they owe for the ship. I keep asking them about it and they keep on saying "It's being dealt with". It's been going on for almost nine years now, and still the State Department legal claims people can only keep on saying "It's being dealt with". The most annoying thing is we all know damn well it isn't being dealt with.'

I went back to the *Penthouse* office after seeing Anderson and there was a message from my CIA contact at Falls Church asking me to return his call. He said, 'I've made arrangements for you to meet a guy who is closely involved with the State Department legal claims. I'm coming into town to see him with you. We'll meet at a bar called the Hawk and the Dove. It's up beyond the Capitol on Pennsylvania Avenue. See you there at eight.'

The man from the State Department was very nervous. We had a beer each, indulged in some post-introduction small talk, then took off for a small pizza house I knew up on Wisconsin Avenue where there was plenty of space between the tables and we could talk freely.

'The main problem over compensation was initially the way the State Department handled claims, but then there started to be threats, and bad feeling on both sides aggravated the situation. I'm not trying to make excuses for the Government because they handled the whole thing badly. But some of the *Liberty* people who by this time had left the navy, started to get very heavy with threats to expose the work *Liberty* was doing off Gaza when the Israelis hit her.

'There were a number of groups formed to help press claims for the *Liberty*. You know them. They were set up with the encouragement of various anti-Zionist groups and pro-Arab lobbyists who wanted to use *Liberty* for their own ends to influence public opinion against Israel and so against Jewish interests here in America. The thing about the *Liberty* incident is that it represented a genuine black mark against Israel and showed up the flaws in America's Middle East policy. So it was a tailor-made piece of dynamite material for the anti-Zionist people to use as a stick to beat the administration with. I don't believe they're so anxious to expose the deals the United States made with Egypt before the 1973 War so there could be a whole about-face policy in the

139

Middle East to phase out the extent of cooperation with Israel and improve ties with the Arabs.

'Anyway, the *Liberty* agitation-groups got round to advising people to use a bit of muscle in their bargaining over compensation and the threats started. You know the thing. "Pay up or we'll tell all." Principally it was to do with the spreading of a rumour that an American submarine was actually underneath *Liberty* at the time of the attack and filmed the whole thing through a periscope or something. Actually there was no submarine anywhere near the area. There were also threats to expose details of *Liberty*'s working brief with the NSA. These sort of threats were fairly common. So the State Department, the FBI, and naval intelligence responded in kind and went through the routine of a little bureaucratic harassment – like frequent IRS and Social Security check-ups – to show the troublemakers there was no future in being tough. Unfortunately the administration couldn't seem to get anyone to put pressure on the Israelis who still owe $7 million for the ship and who just fail to respond to our frequent demands for it. They did answer the first request. They more or less told us where to stick it. They said the *Liberty*'s presence in the area was an aggressive act of war against Israel by the United States, and that America had suffered the consequences of it. They said the matter was closed and, so far as I can see, the American Government has accepted this, rightly or wrongly.'

The State Department man left ahead of us. When he had gone I told my CIA friend that his remark about the submarine was interesting but left it at that. The film from the submarine was a vital but sensitive issue.

Steven McKenna had mentioned an officer from the *Andrew Jackson* leaving Rota for Washington on 14 June, six days after *Liberty* was hit, supposedly carrying a canister of film. Also, accepting that the information so far provided was on the whole fairly accurate, why didn't the State Department man say *Liberty*'s working brief included a close liaison with the USS *Andrew Jackson*, if he wanted to tell all?

I didn't expose my information or my thoughts on this to my friend. The less people knew, the better. The way the State Department lawyer had talked made me suspect he had been pulled out to

140

put over an official line, disguised as confidential revelations. I told my CIA friend I more or less agreed with what the lawyer had to say and that his view gave an important slant to my story. I went back to my hotel, feeling fairly confident I had seen through an attempt to feed me a phoney line to support the administration's so far uncooperative reaction to my proposed story.

My deadline time was now beginning to run out. I had to go back to New York to write up my piece and hand it in to *Penthouse.*

I rechecked into the Sheraton and spent two days closeted in my room on the twenty-third floor writing and re-writing until I had produced a two-part piece with a total of almost 7,000 words. I handed it to Peter Block who told me the articles would appear in the May and June issues of the magazine. He said Guccione wanted to see me.

I made an appointment to go round to Guccione's apartment at seven that night. It was snowing. I couldn't find a cab so I walked to the apartment between Fifth and Madison.

Guccione called me into his living/working quarters. In the centre of the room was a long table. Guccione sat at the head of it, but on the left-hand side. I sat on the right, opposite him. He had a photostat of my story in front of him. He was dressed as always in black shirt and slacks, his shirt open to the waist, his neck festooned with hanging gold chains.

'Pretty good. This should stir up hell with the Israelis. It should create quite an impact. I knew it was a good story when I read the synopsis.'

I agreed that he had been very perceptive, because at the time I gave him the synopsis I had no idea myself that it was anywhere as good as it had now turned out to be.

'When this story breaks we'll get coast-to-coast television and radio coverage. All the newspapers will pick up on it. It's dynamite. Like the story I'm doing now.

'You know anything about drugs? I got this story about this guy who escaped from prison in Mexico where they got him on a phoney drugs rap. He got away by hiding sealed in the gas tank of a car for six days.'

'I hope it was empty,' I said.

141

'Oh sure, some guys drilled holes for him. Must have been pretty uncomfortable: six days in a car's gas tank. Anyway, this guy's writing this story. What are you following the *Liberty* up with?'

'I have the synopsis of a piece about the violence which has been going on at Pine Ridge in South Dakota. The American Indian Movement is very strong there and the Indians claim FBI agents have been coming onto the reservation harassing and murdering people. There have been over a hundred unsolved murders during the last two years.'

'Sounds OK.'

'Yeah. I need some air tickets to go out to Rapid City, South Dakota, and some expenses bread.'

'See Alma Moore, my public relations organizer. Make sure you're back in time for the publication of your articles. Then I want you to go on a coast-to-coast TV tour to publicize them.'

I left New York the following Sunday on a TWA flight to Denver. It was still snowing. At Denver it was warm enough to sit outside, so long as you were sheltered from the wind. I sat for a long time in the sun thinking about *Liberty*; about how much more I could have done and hadn't. I had written just enough to pull together a fairly strong article, but it could have been better. I had left a lot of questions unanswered.

I had not dealt with the alarm over the *Moskva*. I had been unable to get accurate enough information on the movement of the USS *Andrew Jackson*, so I had left all references to the submarine out of the story. And I had not got a copy of the telegram containing the synopsis of the supposed Israeli Court of Inquiry into *Liberty* which had been sent to the State Department from the US Embassy in Tel Aviv. My *Penthouse* story was full of gaps but there were mitigating circumstances. Time had been against me.

The plane to Rapid City was full of the middle American characters I love. They improved my humour almost immediately we left Denver and the mountains and were flying across the broken blue plains heading north across Wyoming and Nebraska to South Dakota. I was free at last.

I had decided to put *Liberty* and all its problems totally behind me until I returned to New York for an appearance on the 'Today'

142

show in early April. Now I just wanted to immerse myself in my new story.

The plane landed at Rapid City in a storm of hail and sleet. The wind was biting cold. I had reserved my usual hire car and the Avis man was at the desk. I signed for a big old Chevy. The office in New York had checked me into a motel just outside town. I decided to by-pass it. I would cut myself off from *Penthouse*, *Liberty*, New York, London, responsibilities, people, telephones, politics, newspapers, everything. I looked at the map. Hot Springs at the foot of the Black Hills looked close enough to the Sioux Reservation at Pine Ridge where I intended to work for a while before moving on to the Cheyenne Reservation on the Tongue River in south-eastern Montana. I checked into the Hot Springs Motel, feeling I had escaped them all.

That night I drove out of the town an hour before sunset, stopped the car on the empty road and then set off walking across the prairie of waving grass. It rose and fell in hilly waves. It was truly like the sea . . . or the desert. The prairie looked and felt much like the Empty Quarter of Qatar and Saudi. I had waited for a long, long time to sit on this empty prairie and consider all the things that had been: the people that had passed this way; the ones that had fought here against nature and Indians; the ones that had died here and the ones that had passed on still further.

On the way back to the car I found an empty cabin, its broken door creaking in the wind. I sat inside on my heels until the light had all but gone. That night I slept well. I planned to sleep late. I felt good. I had not felt so free for a long, long time.

The telephone woke me. I looked at my watch. It was eight. I picked up the hand piece. It had to be a mistake, or the manager with a problem.

'Is that Tony Pearson?'

'Yeah. Who the hell's that?'

'Peter Pringle, *Sunday Times*.'

'Pringle? Jesus, Peter, what the hell're you doing ringing me here? How did you find me?'

Pringle ignored the question.

'Do you know a man called Tito Howard?'

'Sure.'

143

'Do you know he's in jail in Tuscaloosa, Alabama?'

'No! Why's he in jail?'

'Old credit-card forgery charge. He was picked up by the cops. The thing is, he's been involved in some deal in Australia raising money from Iraq for Gough Whitlam. A whole mob of Aussie journalists have been after the story. They've been investigating him and trying to find out about a guy called Harry Fischer.

'Howard gave me a story in Washington last week but the only interview he's given since is from his cell to a local newspaperman. He said he was just about to break a story in *Penthouse* magazine which will be bigger than Watergate. He said he's breaking it in association with you. So I spoke to Peter Block at *Penthouse*. He told me you were doing a story on the Pine Ridge Reservation. So I found you by a process of hotel elimination.'

Pringle was always a crafty schemer.

'Well, Peter, I have written a two-part story on the attack by the Israelis on the USS *Liberty* during the '67 War. It's not a bad piece but hardly "bigger than Watergate". I have no knowledge of Tito's nefarious dealings in Australia, if there have been any. I don't know anything about Harry Fischer, Iraqis, Gough Whitlam, or the Australian political crisis. The only bit I do know is that Tito Howard made a few calls from my apartment to various parts of the world and ran up the phone bill. So far I know less than you. There is nothing in the *Penthouse* pieces in any way connected with Tito's Australian deal. If anything crops up I'll give you a ring. But I don't want a pack of newsmen chasing me all over the Great Plains. I'm trying to work on a sensitive story.'

Pringle promised discretion and rang off.

I put in a call to New York and was told by Peter Block that Tito's claim to be involved in breaking a story 'bigger than Watergate' had drawn a lot of attention from newspapers and radio and TV reporters. Peter then asked me if I knew anything about the *Liberty* attack being photographed from a submarine underneath the ship at the time it was attacked.

I didn't quite know how to deal with that. 'That's just a wild tale,' I said. 'Talk to Pringle at the *Sunday Times* and get him to spin you the rest of the yarn and you will see that allegations about submarines taking pictures through periscopes are small

144

stuff in comparison. The whole tale's rubbish. Just forget about it.'

My late lie-in had been ruined. I showered and drove down to the truckstop on the highway for breakfast. Then I carried on down to Pine Ridge and followed up three contacts with members of the American Indian Movement, who gave me a briefing on the bad security situation at Pine Ridge, which had resulted in the spate of murders.

Driving home that night I noticed the headlights of a car some way behind. The road was otherwise deserted but I kept a watch on the lights. They stayed well behind me. When I reached the highway I signalled right and drove on down to the truckstop for supper. I came out and was unlocking my car when two men sidled out of the shadows.

'Hey you!'

I looked hard at him. 'Don't you bloody Yanks have any manners?'

My English accent surprised the man. I could see he was some sort of plain-clothes cop.

'I'm a Federal Officer. You were seen on Pine Ridge today talking to subversive elements. What's your business there?'

I produced my wallet which contained my Press IDs including a US Army accreditation and a Metropolitan Police press card.

'I'm working on an article for *Penthouse* magazine,' I said.

I heard another man in the shadows say to somebody, 'He's the guy we were supposed to watch out for.'

The officer examining my IDs handed them back. 'I'm sorry to bother you,' he said. 'It's just that we see a lot of funny guys hanging round Pine Ridge. We had three men killed there in a shoot-out last summer. It's bad news. You wanna watch your step there.'

'I will, officer.'

'By the way,' the FBI man said, 'where you stayin'?"

'Hot Springs Motel.'

The man grunted and he got into his car. Two more men came out of the shadows. One got in the front with him. The other climbed into the back. He was carrying a short rifle of some sort. It looked like an M6 carbine or an Armalite. I took the car number. It turned out to be registered to the FBI in Rapid City.

145

Driving out to breakfast next morning, I was pulled in by the local police officer for speeding. I was 10 mph over the limit through his radar, he said. He checked my IDs and the car registration, but was polite and friendly. He already knew who I was. He said he'd seen my car parked outside my cabin. A friend, Peter Parks, had come up from Los Angeles with his girlfriend to meet up with me. The cop had noticed their van. He knew they were with me.

'See your buddies in the blue van with the California plates came up yesterday?'

'Yes.'

'Nice dog that guy has. Wull, sir, sorry to have bothered you. Good luck and have a nice day.'

'Thanks.'

I met up with Peter Parks and his girlfriend Sally at the truck-stop. He told me the cop had looked them over when they arrived but that he had been friendly enough and had chatted idly to them, asking them about me and what I was doing.

Maybe he was just a curious country cop; or maybe the FBI agents in Rapid City had nothing better to do than keep up a surveillance on transient journalists.

A couple of nights later we all went to the house of an Indian friend in the tiny township of Oglalla. We left late so that it was after midnight when I started down the Reservation road towards the main highway.

Just before White Earth River, I saw a car that had been parked along a side track switch on its lights and come after us. They hung behind me for about a mile then started to accelerate. I kicked down hard and wound the Chevy up as far as she would go. The other car also accelerated.

The road from Pine Ridge through the Reservation is pot-holed and full of bad curves. But being used to driving on English country roads which are both narrow and full of bends, I had the advantage over the other car although it was a very small advantage and hard to maintain. I was sweating and cursing, trying to get the Chevy to go faster. In the back, Peter was giving me cool advice about the other car.

'He's coming on faster. He's losing ground. He's coming on fast again.'

Somehow I kept ahead but just as we came up to the highway the pursuer started to gain. There was a Stop sign at the highway junction. I came up to it at close on 120 mph. There was a truck coming fast up the highway to my left. The right was clear. I cut out in a wild screeching turn, burning rubber as I pulled in front of the truck. I heard the trucker's air horn blast out. The other car tried to cut out too. It didn't make it. The driver braked, skidded, did a full ninety-degree turn and went over into the ditch. I kept on driving fast until we were well out of range of pursuit. Then I pulled into the truckstop and parked around the back behind some trailers. We went inside and had some supper while I cooled off. When a decent interval had passed we returned to the motel. God knows what happened to the pursuit car or who the occupants were.

I was up by seven the next morning. I packed and checked out of the motel, telling them I was going back East and leaving my forwarding address at the *Penthouse* Bureau at H Street, Washington. I told Peter and Sally that if they wanted to come on I would meet them at the Sundowner Inn Motel at Forsyth, Montana, and we could go on from there to the Cheyenne Indian Agency at Lame Deer on the Tongue River. Before leaving, I made calls to all the American Indian Movement contacts I had in Rapid City and Pine Ridge. I told them I was going back to Washington. That was for the benefit of the FBI taps they would certainly have on their telephones. Then I set off for Montana via Belle Fourche on the Upper Missouri.

I was bothered by the FBI interest in me. I suspected it had deeper implications than just their concern with my AIM contacts. Two other reporters I knew had been on the Pine Ridge murders story and they had not been pressured or even approached by the FBI. I decided my special case almost certainly related to my being involved with Tito Howard. He had a fat file at the Justice Department. It dealt with his numerous trips abroad and his association with radical Arab nationalists and the PLO. The latest episode as related by Peter Pringle would put Tito in a whole new category if it was true. It seemed Tito had been arrested really on account of the Australian affair. I knew about the supposed credit-card

147

forgeries which had been resolved when Tito repaid the outstanding monies some years ago. The file had probably been lying
dormant with the local police and had been picked up by the FBI in
the course of inquiries and then used as a holding pretext to bring
Howard in for questioning. I was fairly sure that if the FBI could
have pulled me in on some pretext they would have done so. I put
their harassment on and off the reservation down to their attempts
to do this.

Being pursued by the car coming from Oglalla was the clincher.
The men in the car could have been determined criminals set on
robbing and murdering us. On the other hand they could have been
FBI men trying to pull us for being on the Indian Reservation after
midnight which was well within the law for mandatory arrest and
detention for questioning.

If I had been pulled in by the Federal Agents, it would not have
taken long to establish I knew little or nothing about the Tito How-
ard/Harry Fischer business; but I was bothered that they might try
to find out just how much I knew or did not know about the
Liberty business which Tito had freely told police and reporters in
Alabama was 'bigger than Watergate'. The *Penthouse* articles only
contained the bare bones; if I could convince people that was all I
knew it would keep the pressure off me while I continued with a
more detailed investigation. Also enough publicity might have the
result of dragging some interesting people and facts into the open.
Bill Corson had said that the articles might force a re-opening of
official inquiries into the *Liberty* incident and might prove useful in
forcing the release of still-classified material, including the transcripts of the secret sessions of the Senate Foreign Relations Committee and the files on the compensation claims and settlements.

So far I had accused the US Government of helping to start a
war on Egypt, and the Israelis of breaking faith with America,
principally by taking the Jordanian territory of the West Bank and
Old Jerusalem.

I was still mulling over the possibility that the USS *Andrew
Jackson* had been operating covertly with the *Liberty* on a mission,
probably against Israeli missile sites in the Negev Desert, to
prevent the use of long-range missile attacks, nuclear or conventional, on civilian targets.

If confirmed, this information would put a whole new light on American-Israeli relations. It would also help explain the turn of US foreign policy from Israel to the Arab World, as the October War had allegedly proved.

From what I had been told by some dissident Egyptian politicians and general officers, the '73 War had been yet another affair of American manipulation. It had been fought to re-establish Arab morale, but only as far as a compromise position of equal gains to either side, which is why the Egyptians had allowed the Israelis to establish a forward position in the Bitter Lakes area close to Suez. General Shazli had been removed from command of the Egyptian Army because he disagreed with Sadat's plan to fight to achieve a compromise stand from which to negotiate. Being a loyal officer, Shazli has never discussed his disagreement with Sadat, but some of his supporters told me he felt confident he could have recaptured Sinai after his initial crossing of the Canal. The forward movement of the Egyptian Army was halted by special order from Sadat, who had received an American appeal to avoid a desperate confrontation with Israel which might trigger the reaction of missiles against civilian targets they had feared in 1967 if the same circumstances occurred. The State Department had told Sadat that the Israelis would never negotiate from a position of defeat. So the war ended in a stand-off; and Henry Kissinger was able to set about negotiating his great Middle Eastern peace which everyone hoped would not be a facsimile of his great Far Eastern peace settlement which precipitated the appalling loss of life in Vietnam before and during the American withdrawal.

Privately, both State Department and NSA people, including Kissinger, endorsed the opinion of General Shazli that the problem of Israel and the Arab world could only be solved by the total military defeat of the Israelis. Since the Israelis had plutonium and would never allow defeat, preferring to indulge in a sort of one-sided suicide pact in which they blew everyone to pieces including themselves, the Americans and the Russians had to play the game carefully around them to avoid World War III. They never forgot that Holocaust, together with Diaspora, was the word best guaranteed to change the emotional spirit of Jews everywhere. Nuclear war was probably more meaningful to Jews than to any

149

other people. It held religious significance.

This was a whole new aspect of the Middle East confrontation situation which stood up to a much closer investigation. So I needed to keep *Andrew Jackson* under wraps. I had to watch Tito Howard. He had already given out the 'submarine' fact to the local Birmingham, Alabama, newspapermen, who might or might not feed it to the AP wire. But if they did, without any sort of corroboration or substance, the AP wouldn't pursue it themselves. They would drop the story. If I was asked about it I would continue to say it was pure fancy.

Chapter Eleven

I spent almost two uneventful weeks in Montana at Coalstrip, a mining town twenty miles north-east of Lame Deer. I then flew back to New York and on Monday 2 April, at five-thirty a.m., Guccione's publicist, Sherwood Ross, came round to escort me to the NBC-TV studios on Sixth Avenue to appear on the 'Today' show at seven. I was to be interviewed about my *Penthouse* articles by Barbara Walters and Jim Hartz.

The previous day had been spent travelling and the evening and night had passed pleasantly and easily at Nanni's restaurant where I had consumed the best part of a bottle and a half of Frascati.

It was very cold walking across to Sixth Avenue but it did little to revive me. I needed another three hours' sleep. I didn't have a hangover, not a real hangover. I was just tired.

At the studio they put some make-up on my wine-drawn face and gave me cups of black coffee, one after another. Sherwood Ross kept on telling me not to forget to mention Guccione and *Penthouse* at every opportunity. When I tried to pull my ideas together I couldn't even remember the more intimate details of the damned story.

After the news bulletin I was ushered on into the glare of the lights. I felt stupid. Guccione had insisted I wear a jacket and tie. Jim Hartz smiled but Barbara Walters looked grim. They introduced me. They started to explain my story. Barbara Walters asked some question about the background and dully I started to recite the stuff about the CIA dealing with the Israelis and so on and so on. Then Barbara Walters suddenly said, 'We spoke to General Dayan yesterday [he was in New York raising cash for Israeli war bonds], and he denied your allegations. He said it was all nonsense.'

I should have said, 'What the hell did you expect him to say?' Any other answer from the man would have been like Nixon going on network television and admitting to personally burgling the Watergate.

Instead I grunted incoherently. There was a map of the 1967 War area. It was a rotten map. It was set up on an easel like a school blackboard. They were using it to try to explain my story to the viewers. They didn't seem to be doing too well.

Jim Hartz then hit me with a question about a suggestion in my piece that *Liberty* could have been hit by Russian carrier-borne aircraft. 'That was impossible,' he said. 'The Russians did not have a carrier in the Mediterranean in 1967.'

Which was true. I was irritated enough to have floored him with the stuff about the *Moskva* and the NATO assessment that the Russians had not only perfected the Yak 36 jump jet, but had already put it into service and had been sending two wings to the war area in the *Moskva*. And even if the Yak assessment was wrong, the *Moskva* could carry up to thirty Hormone anti-submarine helicopters, the Russian tactical answer to Polaris. That was the significant thing. There was really no need for an alarm about jump jets. But, without explaining about *Andrew Jackson*, it was impossible to explain why an anti-Polaris-submarine cruiser was so vital at that moment and why it was not impossible that a Russian airborne attack could have been launched against *Liberty*.

All this didn't flash through my mind in a second. I just reasoned dully that Hartz was right to pick me up on this but there was no way I could reply. I said something stupid like, 'Really, I didn't know that,' and the interview floundered on through a series of questions to which I recited too-long, boring answers from the article. Except for the brief respite of the commercial breaks during which Walters, Hartz and I sat in embarrassed silence, the ordeal continued for thirty minutes.

When I got off, Sherwood Ross said, 'You were awful. They made mincemeat of you. I don't know if Guccione will want you to go on the coast-to-coast circuit now.' He sounded disappointed.

Thank God, I thought. All I wanted now was lots of coffee, a big plate of eggs and corn-beef hash and a shortstack of pancakes and syrup.

Sherwood had arranged a press conference for me at the Washington National Press Club at midday.

He hurried us through breakfast, piled me into his Cadillac and set off for Washington breaking the 55 mph speed limit the whole way.

152

I didn't feel any better when we arrived but I climbed onto the rostrum and stared over the lines of chairs in front of me. Sherwood had hired a fairly large room. I thought, if I was part of the Washington Press Club I would not bother to come to pick up some other reporter's crummy story. I was surprised when they did start to file in but most surprised when Tito Howard himself appeared, flanked by some of his cohorts from the various pro-Arab lobbies and Arab information groups. He had come, he told me, to sit in with me during the press conference. Sherwood persuaded him it wasn't such a good idea.

Before the conference started, Howard was talking about making public the startling 'new' revelation that an American submarine had photographed, perhaps even filmed, the whole attack on *Liberty*. I persuaded him that now was not the time to introduce a new factor into the story. It was better to leave it until later, to 'revive' the story if necessary. He agreed. I had explained to Sherwood who Howard was and how the FBI were in close contact trying to find out what had happened to Mr H. Fischer. Alarmed that *Penthouse* might get tainted by the strange saga of the Australian affair and by the inference that the story was anti-Semitic in principle because of the appearance of various anti-Zionist group representatives with Tito Howard, Sherwood went off to find the National Press Club bouncer.

Tito was hurt. He said the story had been his idea and now he was being pushed out of it. I told him this was not true. I just did not want *Liberty* to be tainted by political motives.

Bob Guccione had decided to go ahead with the coast-to-coast TV appearances and promotion of the story despite the 'Today' Show farce. So the whirlwind began and I became more and more embroiled in the issue of ethnic loyalties. My story made me either a religious or racial bigot or both. The TV and radio interviewers were either pro-Israeli (Los Angeles, New York) or pro-Arab (Huston, Atlanta). The pro-Israel people invariably accused me of being anti-Semitic. After a while I didn't even bother to argue with them. They were too ignorant to know different or better.

At Atlanta I cut the TV tour off. I was supposed to go on to Chicago, Philadelphia, Boston and God knows where else. I was sick of talking about *Liberty* and sick of being accused and mis-understood by stupid men who knew nothing about the Middle East. They believed the Israelis were the embattled heroes and that three million homeless, often starving Palestinian refugees were all bloody butchers running through the world killing poor innocent Jews with their Russian Kalachnikovs and bloody Muslim swords. To these people, the chequered Arab kaffiyah was like the black-on-red swastika of Hitler's Storm Troopers. I thought, 'If only they knew the truth.' But they did not want to know the truth. In the Middle East, truth is a broken sword of justice.

When I started the TV tour I lost contact with Tito Howard. I went home in May, disenchanted with everything I had done.

Summer went and autumn came. I had just enough cash left either to pay off my bills and go broke or make a trip to Africa where I knew there was a chance to get into the guerilla camps in Mozambique and maybe come out with a story and pictures that would double my £1,000 investment. It didn't work. I sneaked into Mozambique through a back-door route, managed to get one piece out of it for the *Sunday Times*, and then quit.

I arrived back at Cheyne Place just in time to be evicted from my flat for non-payment of rent. I was rescued by a friend and neighbour, an ex-cavalry officer called Peter Grant. I moved in with him, sleeping on the floor of his living room.

In February *Africa* magazine carried a story accusing the press in general and me in particular of trying to 'de-stabilize' Mozam-bique by spreading malicious rumours about its social and economic condition. Also, the article said, there was no record of my ever being in the country. They implied I had entered secretly and illegally which was only partly true, and only then because the Mozambique Government had repeatedly refused to answer my cables from Nairobi requesting a visa. The article went on to further imply I worked for 'outside agencies', which meant the CIA. In view of my work on *Liberty* my relations, official and unofficial, with the CIA were not the most cordial.

Since returning to London after the publication of the *Liberty* piece in *Penthouse* I had been approached by Arabs from various embassies, obviously acting on behalf of their intelligence services and inquiring as to the whereabouts of Harry Fischer.

154

Their version of the Whitlam story was this.

The CIA needed the Australian government to renegotiate the continued American use of an electronics surveillance station at Pine Gap, near Canberra. Gough Whitlam did not approve of the CIA's active presence in his country and refused to renew the agreement. So the CIA organized a scandal to get Whitlam dismissed by using agents provocateurs with close associations with the Arabs to raise loans for the Labour Party on the pretext of its pro-Arab, and particularly its pro-Palestinian, stand.

Somewhere in this tangled web appeared Harry Fischer and Tito Howard. Fischer was a known Palestinian fund-raiser. He was a friend of Rupert Murdoch. Soon after Whitlam began raising Arab cash, Murdoch's papers broke the story and the Governor-General sacked the Labour Government.

Here the story should end. But it goes on. Refusing to surrender, Whitlam raised more capital. Again the deal was shopped to Murdoch but this time there was no doubt where the information came from. Howard admitted that Fischer went to Murdoch 'because Harry Fischer really wanted to get Whitlam's deputy, the trade-union leader and alleged Zionist, Bob Hawke'.

The Iraqis were upset about this, the Arab diplomats told me. They thought Tito Howard had been duped and was innocent of intrigue, but Fischer was known to the Iraqi secret service as a CIA officer. Since he had, to their mind, defrauded them of a large sum of money to discredit the good friend of Arab nationalism, Gough Whitlam, he had also made fools of them and they were angry and anxious to lay hands on him to extract some explanation.

Fischer was afraid of both the Iraqis and Murdoch, Tito Howard said. He thought someone was out to kill him. He was not quite sure who.

Howard said he had a number of meetings with Murdoch who offered him $20,000 for the *Liberty* story and $20,000 to film Gough Whitlam through a two-way mirror accepting more Arab money, if Howard could arrange it. This sounded a little dramatic but it was not out of the general style of cheque-book journalism practised by Murdoch's newspapers. This modus operandi helped earn him his 'dirty digger' tag.

This story concerned me only because Tito Howard on a number of occasions did say there was $20,000 available from Murdoch on *Liberty* if I needed it; but these offers began back in 1975, before and during the original Whitlam crisis in November, but well before the February 1976 crisis. I am therefore only assuming – Howard has never suggested it – that Fischer and he had contracted with Murdoch during the original Arab scandal in the summer of 1975, and the February 1976 affair was a continuation of this contract.

I only told the Arabs I had been questioned by the press in America about the incident but I knew very little of its background. I did not know Harry Fischer and I did not have any information as to his whereabouts. The Arab/CIA tale was plausible enough, but as far as I knew there was no connection between Fischer and the CIA and if there was it was not my business and anyhow the story was dead. If the Iraqi secret service wanted to turn over Harry Fischer I was sure they could do it without bothering me. I was sure Tito Howard would help them if and when he reappeared. I then forgot the matter.

In a desperate attempt to raise finance I next attempted to launch an entertainments magazine based in concept on *New York* and *New West*. Amazingly, I got response and initial capital and the project was just about to be launched when two pieces appeared on successive nights in the Londoner's Diary of the London *Evening Standard*. The first poked fun at the magazine idea. The second was an unprovoked and vicious attack on me.

Ironically, or perhaps significantly, *Liberty* saved me. Peter Grant and I had moved to a new, larger flat in Redesdale Street, Chelsea, and I came home two weeks after the failure of my magazine to find a message that Quartet Books were interested in a book on the *Liberty* incident. Almost simultaneously but purely coincidentally with the signing of the book contract, Tito Howard arrived in London on his way to Paris and Iraq.

His life had disintegrated much like mine. His marriage had broken up and his home in Beirut had been destroyed during the civil war. His deal with Harry Fischer had produced little cash.

Howard's own fortunes seemed to be still on the slide, but he was going off to Iraq, Kuwait, Dubai and to Libya where his film

'Kuneitra – Death of a City' was still in demand. He told me of one of his French contacts, an ex-Foreign Legion paratroop officer who now lived in the Arab quarter of Montmartre. This man, who seemed to have a close and unusual working knowledge of the Israeli Intelligence Service's anti-PLO operations, warned me that the Israelis knew I had a contract for a book on *Liberty* and that they were 'better than interested' in the project. An Israeli female agent had been trying to get into Tito Howard's Paris operation by making up to him, but her cover had been blown by the ex-paratrooper's Algerian girlfriend. The Israelis still seemed anxious about the *Liberty* story. Their reaction to the original *Penthouse* article had been mute. Apart from one invitation to lunch from an Israeli quasi-government official, a man who has always proved a sincere and honest contact, soon after I returned from the States in May 1976, I had experienced no overt response to my work from apparent Israeli sources. I had received one strange telephone call from a 'Jack Burnyar' who vaguely told a friend of mine – he did not contact me directly – that he had 'read my stuff' in the *Manchester Evening News* and wanted to talk to me about a story'. He left a contact number in the City. I rang it just before the Easter holiday and he said the story was 'something to do with the Middle East' but would not be specific. A week later I telephoned him again, said I couldn't do the story and would pass it to a friend. I then asked Nick Davies, now Foreign Editor at the *Daily Mirror*, to check the man out. Davies called him: 'Burnyar' refused to give details of the story over the telephone and told Nick he would call back. He never did.

Three weeks after this incident Neville Player, the deputy editor of *Penthouse* in London, told me that the Fulham office of Allan Radnor, then the magazine's London editor, had been burgled. A filing cabinet containing articles had been forced open; the only article missing was one I had written in February on international terrorist groups and the growing cooperation between them. I had been helped with this research by Mr Eldon, the Israeli Press Attaché in Paris.

If there was any significance in the theft from *Penthouse*, it escaped me. I had been commissioned by my publisher to continue research into the *Liberty*. So I returned, in May, to the United

States, working out of an apartment I had rented in Alexandria, Virginia.

The first thing I picked up when I arrived in Washington was a piece written recently as a syndication column by Jack Anderson, which once more raised the question of why the Israelis had still failed to pay the $7 million they owed the US Government for *Liberty*. I rang the State Department and asked them for a comment. A press office spokesman said the Department of State didn't really know what to do. The matter was periodically submitted to the Israelis and the Israelis ignored it. That was how it had gone on for ten years and was likely to go on until the State Department gave up trying to collect.

I rang the Navy PR people to find out if they had received any more information on the supposed Israeli Court of Inquiry into *Liberty* as a result of my *Penthouse* articles. They hadn't. I spoke to the officers I had dealt with in late 1975 and early 1976. They seemed distant and cautious, but not hostile. They responded like men under pressure. I was told my requests for more detailed transcripts of naval evidence would be considered and my calls returned. They were not. I never expected they would be. I didn't need the detailed transcripts. I already had access to adequate evidence. I had tested the climate of reaction. It was frosty. I would need to find out why.

I rang Mrs Toth's number at Virginia Beach. A man answered. Mrs Toth was away in Europe for the summer. I then made another call to a lawyer at the State Department.

'Jesus. Are you back again asking more questions?'

'Right. Did my piece in *Penthouse* produce any reaction in your department on the compensation issue? Has anyone found any records of payments or papers relating to degrees of compensation, qualification for payments and all that stuff?'

'Look, buddy, you caused a lot of trouble with those pieces in *Penthouse*. They knew I'd talked. I'm lucky I've still got my job. Now leave me alone!'

I rang Mrs Toth's lawyer, McWater; I got a clerk or some junior partner. 'Look, we told you all the files related to Captain Toth and the others have been destroyed. Mr McWater's not available. There is no more to say!'

I had believed they were on my side but I had obviously miscalculated.

I now telephoned a former officer of the *Liberty*.

He was pleased to see me and excited at the idea of a book on the incident. There was still a lot to say. He had a friend at the State Department who had some new evidence in the form of confidential telegrams between the US Embassy in Tel Aviv and Washington. I had been trying to get my hands on these for some time. They went to confirm facts I already knew, many of them already included in the original *Penthouse* articles. None of them concerned the USS *Andrew Jackson*.

My first approach to the collection of that information was a nominal request to the US Navy for confirmation that a Polaris submarine put into Rota, Spain, on or about 12 June 1967. If such a submarine did put into Rota on a relevant date, did an officer leave it, and was he logged taking urgent air transportation to Washington? Was he carrying a bonded diplomatic package? How long had the submarine been on patrol?

The answers came quickly. The USS *Andrew Jackson* had put into Rota on 14 June. She had left that port on 2 June for a 'routine patrol on temporary Sixth Fleet attachment'. A Lieutenant-Commander was logged as taking urgent transportation from the US Air Force base to Washington. He was carrying classified material. What or how much was not on record.

Could a submarine like the *Jackson* have surfaced and engaged motor torpedo boats in conventional combat? I asked.

No, I was told. To engage motor torpedo boats at close quarters would be irregular and inadvisable. If I was referring to the circumstances of the attack on the USS *Liberty* (they had guessed the direction of my questioning) then I should realize a submarine like the *Andrew Jackson* would have been helpless to interfere on the *Liberty*'s behalf without severely endangering herself. Also, a Polaris submarine can only act on the initiative of its fleet commander, not on its own initiative. In the circumstances of the *Liberty* incident even Admiral Martin on the USS *Little Rock* would have needed confirmation from the US Naval Forces Commander Europe, Admiral McCain, before issuing orders for the *Andrew Jackson* to take appropriate action. Otherwise a submarine could only 'observe'.

Was it correct that a Polaris submarine had a facility to observe through its periscope with a camera turret containing a zoom lens with a considerable long-focus facility?

Yes, I was told, that was correct. A Polaris could observe and record its observations on film.

Had that happened in the case of the *Liberty*?

'I am not authorized to say. I do not have that information. It is not available,' the naval voice told me.

'Hold on. Just answer me a hypothetical question. If the USS *Andrew Jackson* happened to be in the immediate vicinity of the USS *Liberty* when she was attacked and there was no way she could aid *Liberty*, was it likely the Captain would have filmed the attack with his camera observation facility?'

'He sure would. Probably in technicolor.'

'Who would have more specific details?'

'Not me. I'm only an ex-Lieutenant-Commander. Tell you what, though. I'll give you a number to ring in the Pentagon. The guy there is a general officer. He was sort of tickled by your *Penthouse* pieces. He thought they were damned good. You talk to him about it. OK?'

'Thanks. Maybe I can buy you a drink sometime.'

'Mr Pearson, you ain't ever met me, don't know me and you never will. I bet you've even forgotten my name?'

'Yes.'

'OK. Good luck.'

The general's aide answered when I rang the number the ex-Lieutenant-Commander had given me. He seemed to be expecting my call. He told me arrangements had been made to see his chief. Could I go to a certain number block at the Pentagon complex at ten the next morning and ask the security officer for him. He would escort me to the general's office.

I took a cab to the Pentagon from my apartment. I thought maybe it was better that my own car wasn't seen around the Pentagon's parking lots.

I went, as told, to the door and the officer, as promised, escorted me in to his chief.

The chief could have been the perfect Hollywood caricature of a tough Pentagon general, but when he spoke his faintly Southern accent was soft and steady. He complimented me on my *Penthouse* articles and I explained my book commission. I outlined various points in the story where there were still gaps but asked particularly for clarification on these issues:

Why was the *Andrew Jackson* with *Liberty* and was it true she had been briefed to attack and destroy Israeli missile bases if so ordered?

Was it true the *Jackson* had filmed the entire *Liberty* attack with her underwater-to-surface surveillance gear and, if so, was such film or parts of it available?

Why had all the communications sent to the *Liberty* gone missing? What had the navy inquiry into this mysterious incident produced?

Why had the *Liberty* been told to expect the Russian cruiser *Moskva* in her immediate area 'imminently' when the *Moskva* was still with the Black Sea Fleet? And why had the NSA warned the White House and the State Department that the *Moskva* was carrying 'jump jets' when she was only carrying the KA 5 Hormone anti-submarine helicopter?

'It seems to me,' I said, 'that the implied threat of the *Moskva*, if it existed, was against *Andrew Jackson* rather than *Liberty* but the warnings issued by the NSA implied a threat to *Liberty* of a possible air attack by Soviet fighters. Of all the wild contentions made about the attack on the *Liberty* this is the craziest.'

The general paused for a moment after I finished my outline of questions. Then he began: 'OK. Let's take the first, and remember that I never told you any of this stuff.

'A Polaris submarine had been ordered to reinforce the Sixth Fleet force for a number of reasons but mainly because the Soviets had pushed two Echo-class missile subs into the Med at the beginning of June. The movement of the subs involved the *Moskva* business, but I'll deal with that as a separate answer.

'Before the Israelis attacked Egypt it had been considered that something could go wrong even though we were ninety per cent convinced the Israelis would win – and win quickly. Ninety per cent convinced is a lot. But there was still ten per cent of doubt and that ten per cent contained the possibility that if the Israelis were pushed with their backs to the sea they would operate their Doomsday plan to launch a fullscale missile attack against Baghdad, Cairo and Damascus. Some people in the NSA figured this could even be a limited nuclear attack as the Israelis did have the capability. But that would have been unlikely unless they wanted to kill themselves too. The targets were too close to Israel for the Israelis to avoid the effects of fall-out which even from a limited nuclear warhead would be pretty extensive.

'But even if an attack had been made using missiles with conventional warheads it would have provoked a Soviet response. The Soviets had told us quite frankly that any attempt by Israel to escalate the war to include the bombardment of civilian targets would meet with instant reprisals from their forces. They had the capability. There were fighter/bomber bases in Iraq where Soviet pilots were available to fly combat missions, and there was a major Soviet assault base near Sofia in Bulgaria. They knew we had told the Israelis there was absolutely no way US troops could be used to support them, and US forces would not engage in open hostility with the Soviets over the issue of an attack against Israel. To do so would have been insane whatever bullshit the White House gave out. Of course the possibility of the Israelis escalating the war would have involved us, like it or not, for general NATO strategic reasons. If the Soviets had attacked Israel in retaliation for Israeli missile strikes we would have had to intervene. We didn't want to and the Soviets didn't want to force us to. So we drew up a contingency plan with the Russians.

'If the war moved in any direction towards missile escalation we, as wards of Israel, would personally knock out all the Israeli missile sites and bomber assault bases and even airborne bombers to prevent the Soviets having to do it and to avoid confrontation. To effect this policy we needed eyes and ears close to the fighting. There was no way the normal intelligence networks could be trusted because of Israeli infiltration. We needed a monitoring base close to. So *Liberty* was sent in. It was impossible to use aerial reconnaissance and electronic activity centres like an Orion P3, a B52 or a U2 because of the high degree of aerial combat and the implications if a US Air Force plane was shot down by a Russian or Arab fighter or missile. If an intelligence ship was able to monitor an escalation of the war, among many other surveillance duties, we would need a close attack base to hit the Israeli sites. From just off the Gaza coast we were in ample range of even the most southerly Israeli sites in the Negev. The computers on a Polaris sub can pinpoint and preselect target and range so that on an attack order the reaction and application of the attack is both instantaneous and accurate. In thirty minutes we could have knocked out every effective Israeli missile site. A submarine had to be used in such a plan because of its concealment capability. To avoid detection it could not use its monitoring gear. That was *Liberty*'s role.

'Now about the filming of the *Liberty* attack. Stuff like that is the province of the NSA and whatever I think about those guys I can't breach their security. My own view is, such a film was taken, it was used in inquiries to show the attack on *Liberty* was deliberate and that the ship was in international waters, which the Israelis never disputed, plainly showing US Navy markings and American colours. Indignation aside, I must say that if the Israelis were aware of the circumstances of our total plan, General Dayan had good reasons for ordering the strike against *Liberty*. It was still an act of war against an ally, but soldiers fight wars and work out their strategy for practical, not sentimental, reasons. However, I don't believe the Israelis knew the full implications of *Liberty*'s orders and her role. I think they hit her simply to stop the ship passing the information to Washington that the Israeli Army was overrunning Jordanian territory in contravention of every agreement made with the US Government and was planning to escalate the war, despite the UN call for a ceasefire, attack Syria and overrun the Golan. Attacking the *Liberty* to help along this land-grabbing was a premeditated and devious act of back-stabbing. It was an act of military foolhardiness and in international law, one of deliberate piracy. Of course the Israelis constantly make fools of us when they can, which isn't much now because 'the people who matter in the Pentagon won't have it any more.

'On the communications to *Liberty* matter, I can't help you much. Inquiries were made. They establish the messages were sent and they were designated "pinnacle" which is A1 priority. They were mis-routed from the NSA and filed away when they returned

163

there. The NSA weeded out quite a few persons after the inquiry but no charges were made or disciplinary action taken against anybody. My own view is that the close cooperation of the CIA with Israeli intelligence had reached such a peak in 1967 that our whole intelligence network was thick with people involved in that cooperation – not necessarily Israeli agents – just guys who were helping along the close cooperation of the Agency and Mossad.'

'You're saying the Israelis, or someone helping them, deliberately mislaid the cables to prevent *Liberty* leaving the area before she could be attacked and destroyed with all her information?'

'That's about it. But there is no material evidence to support this idea.'

'Could you relate the same situation to the *Moskva* cables, then? Could they have been sent to cause a deliberate Soviet alarm which could have been later used as an excuse if the *Liberty* attack had been successful, the ship sunk and all her crew killed?'

'Could have been. The NSA say the estimation of the *Moskva*'s movements had been premature and was based on confused NATO reports and misleading intelligence from Soviet penetration. But the Sixth Fleet knew *Moskva* was about to move to the Med as she did in September, so when the reports about her coming through the Bosporus started flying around there was every reason to believe they were accurate. There was a war going on, the Soviets were backing one of the factions fighting in it and so it was not strategically unlikely they would move in an anti-Polaris sub cruiser and a couple of destroyers to back up the two Soviet Echo missile subs which were already on the scene. I think the only people who really believed the jump-jet threat were damned silly politicians. The Soviets didn't have the Yak 36 in service in 1967. We knew that. And there was no chance they would put any of their land-based fighters into the area. If the *Moskva* had moved into the Med it could have been argued that its Hormone helicopters, which fire missiles and carry depth charges, could have attacked and sunk *Liberty*. But if the *Liberty* had gone down and someone tried to plant the blame on the Soviets they would have had to say the ship had been torpedoed by a Russian sub. The size and shape of the torpedoes on the Israeli MTBs is almost identical to the fish carried on Echo subs. The only flaw in that explanation would have come to light when the sunken *Liberty* was examined by an underwater team. They would have seen all the bullet holes and rocket and cannon shell holes which were proof of an air attack. So, to put the blame on the Soviets, someone somewhere had to produce Soviet aircraft, although even then I don't know how they would have explained away the ammunition used against *Liberty*. It would be NATO-issue stuff, not Soviet unless the Israelis had rearmed their Mirages to fire Soviet rockets, cannon shells and machine-gun bullets, which is possible but unlikely. Going back to your question the short answer is, the *Moskva* could have been a deliberate false alarm but was most likely, almost certainly, rather a typical US/NATO intelligence foul-up. As you probably saw from Watergate our intelligence people produce the absolute tops in all-American foul-ups. They're the biggest and the best. That answer your questions, boy?'

'Yes, thank you, sir.'

'Don't mention it, son. I mean that. I mean, don't you mention where the hell you got this from.'

'I won't. I'll say it came from a general in the Pentagon.'

'Goddam it. There are enough of the useless bastards hanging around here to blame it on. Well, good luck, son. Keep your head down. The sort of work you did makes you bad enemies and in this murky game of hide and seek folks play dirty.'

Chapter Twelve

Tito Howard flew into Washington from Paris three days after the interview.

I stayed around with him, first in Georgia and then in Florida, and in September I returned to London to work on the first draft of the book. By this time the publishers had announced its coming publication in their catalogue. Four weeks after it appeared, the Chelsea flat I shared with my friend Peter Grant was burgled during the weekend. I was down on the Kent coast. Peter rang me when he arrived home on the Sunday, to say the place had been ransacked, probably the previous night. But the only obvious thing, stolen had been a box containing a gold tiepin and his regimental cuff links.

My brief bag containing an assortment of papers had been turned out on the carpet and the contents searched.

Inexplicably, the burglars had left behind a portable TV set, some valuable prints and paintings, some pieces of valuable jewellery, my gold cigarette lighter and full box of Havana cigars! They had taken selected papers. These were: papers on the growth of South Yemen as a terrorist base, written in French; a full transcript of Captain McGonagle's evidence to the naval court of inquiry into *Liberty*; a summary of the *Liberty* inquiry; a full crew list; a full casualty list; a list of decorations and citations to officers and crew; a copy of an internal State Department memo on the Israeli Court of Inquiry; and a list of names and telephone numbers of the principals involved in the original *Penthouse* story.

The vital material – my notes on the *Andrew Jackson* and the transcript of my interview with the general – I had kept constantly with me until I could write them up and hand them to my publishers.

Peter told me there was no sign of forced entry into the apartment. The lights had been switched off at the mains. Every single light came on when Peter threw the master switch. The curtains were all drawn, but the floor of the living room was littered with spent matches. If the burglars had drawn the curtains to use the lights why had they thrown the main power switch and searched the place by match light, as indicated by the spent matches? Maybe they had been disturbed, had switched off the lights and continued in match light. But the neighbours had seen no one and heard nothing. Our apartment was the only one entered in the block. Who had entered the flat was uncertain, but there was no doubt why. And where had they got my address? The publishers knew it. Tito Howard knew it. A couple of Arab embassies knew it. The burglars must have known there was never anyone in the flat on Saturday. I packed my bags and left London for the country, telling no one where I was going. The knowledge someone had of Peter's and my movements indicated a close-order surveillance.

I had been gone two weeks when Peter telephoned and said two people who sounded 'dodgy' and refused to identify themselves had telephoned asking for me. He said I wasn't around. They then asked if Peter had a forwarding address or telephone number. He said no. A day later Peter rang again. Howard had telephoned to say he was coming to London and could I meet him at the address in Fulham.

Tito Howard was very edgy. He said the apartment he used in Washington had been entered and searched but nothing had been taken; and his apartment in Beirut had been ransacked. Considering the state of hostilities between Christians, Palestinians, Muslim Leftists and the Syrian Army in Beirut, it was hard to draw a sinister significance from the break-in there. The Washington apartment was owned and occupied by an Israeli, a former major of Bethsheba who was now alienated from the Israeli Government and devoted his time to virulent anti-Zionist activities. It was possible someone might want to turn over Haibe Shreiber in case he was involved in the *Liberty* project, but it was unlikely.

I did not believe the IIS, if they were responsible for the break-in at my apartment, could really believe there would be anything of importance in Washington. Still, perhaps they thought it was worth their time to check it out.

I was now getting very nervous. I did not mind opposition just so long as I could see it or feel it. The unknown, the intangible was just sinister. I had also discovered there had been a short surveillance on the last address I had while working for the *Manchester Evening News*, which was also the last address the Israeli Embassy had for me.

I was assuming this was the Israelis. There were no other interested parties. I told Howard I would try to resolve the matter.

Next day I put in a call to a contact at the Foreign Office. The same afternoon I had a suprise caller.

'Tony. This is Steven McKenna.'

'Steven. I thought you were still in the Gulf.'

'Service ran out, old boy. I have now gone into semi-retirement, working for Her Majesty's Security Services. Brian has left now but the message was passed on to me. You have a problem?'

'Yes.'

'Right, see you in an hour. Whereabouts?'

'Brian used to meet me in the lobby of the Cumberland Hotel by the news-stand.'

'Tell you what. See you at five in the lobby of the hotel at Charing Cross Station, the one at the front of the station. We can have a drink and then I can dash off down to the country. I'm on the old nine-to-five commuter stuff; pin-striped suit, umbrella and all that, with a small army pension on the side.'

Brian had always been precise. McKenna was ten minutes late – 'Couldn't get a cab, old man.'

We found a quiet corner in the bar and sat down with two large gin and tonics.

'Someone burgled my flat. They stole all the papers on the *Liberty* I had there and Peter's regimental cuff links.'

'Bit odd, stealing cuff links.'

'And a tie pin.'

'Nothing else of value?'

'No.'

'What regiment was Peter in?'

'13/18th Hussars.'

'Not easy to get rid of, inscribed regimental cuff links. Not easy to hock cavalry stuff anyway. Were his initials engraved on them?'

'Yes.'

'Who do you think was responsible?'

'Jewish intelligence.'

168

'Possible. Was the break-in very obvious? Did they take anything to make it look like a regular job?'

'Nothing, other than the cuff links and tie pin. They left some valuable stuff.'

'Did you have anything which might have been prejudicial to the Israelis which is still secret? Because in the present state of political play with America they're mighty sensitive.'

'I had all the stuff on the *Andrew Jackson*.'

'All of it?'

'All of it.'

'Well, that would be sensitive enough material to set alarm bells going. Who knew about it?'

'Only the people I dealt with immediately in Washington at the Navy Department and the Pentagon.'

'Anyone in the CIA know about it?'

'I don't know. Maybe.'

'Did any of your friends know about your chum Tito Howard, the Australian affair chap?'

'No. He only knew I was investigating the submarine rumour. Anyway, Tito is honest in that respect. He's one of my best friends.'

'Wasn't suggesting anything to the contrary, old man. Just checking who knew what. Anyway, it isn't all that important. The Jews must know you're doing the book, and there are a thousand and one ways they can find out just what you've come up with. I told you in Nairobi you would get the *Jackson* stuff if you tried. Need any more help now?'

'No thanks, Steven. I only need a bit of back-up from you if necessary.'

'Don't see how I can be of real help, old boy. Unless you have categorical proof that the IIS broke into your flat and pinched your papers, there is no way HMG can make representations to the Israeli Embassy who control the buggers. Even if you did have proof, you would have to present it through the proper channels which would be the Met Police for starters, then the Special Branch. You can talk to whatever contacts you have at the Branch, but they'll only tell you the same thing I've told you. If you're worried about the IIS, forget it. All the stuff you hear about people getting bumped off

169

in dark alleys is rot. Maybe they do it to the poor old PLO men, but on this patch they keep their noses clean. There's no love lost between the security services and the Israeli Mossad and if they step out of line here they're back to Tel Aviv, post haste.

'If you're really worried, old man, I should take a long holiday in Hong Kong or somewhere suitably far away but within the jurisdiction of what few of your chums remain in the old British raj. New Zealand would be a good spot. You would be OK there.'

McKenna's humour was archaic and Fifth Form, but he was concerned. He was a good friend and he was trying to help.

'Seriously, I would just get your stuff written as soon as possible and hand it in to your publisher. Once he's got it there's really no reason for anyone to bother you. If they did, it would be the old business of bolting the stable door after the horse has shoved off.'

'Thanks, Steven.'

'OK.'

He walked towards his platform. It was the last time I would see him.

'And remember,' he said, 'lots of sex and violence and you'll make a million. Good luck, old man.'

Three months later he returned to the Gulf with a group of ex-21 SAS men. He was killed in a helicopter accident.

Bearing in mind McKenna's advice, I talked with Tito Howard over the possibility of going to Florida to work on the book. He thought I would do better to go to Egypt. Haki, the Egyptian Press Attaché in Washington, had promised to arrange a trip to Cairo. I followed it up with Dr Mustafah Mounier, the Press Attaché in London, and he quickly made arrangements for me with Cairo.

On Friday, 28 October, I arranged to leave London on the following afternoon by the 2 p.m. Egypt Air flight. Dr Mounier asked me to take some papers for him and hand them to a colleague at the Information Ministry. Everything was arranged. At seven that night I received a call on the ex-directory line Howard and I now used in the Fulham apartment. It was a PLO friend.

'Don't make the trip to Egypt. Things there are very bad.'

'Why?'

'There is much happening. Sadat has big plans with the Israelis and

170

there is going to be trouble amongst the Arabs. The people at Al Rasd [Fatah intelligence] think it is dangerous to go there. They heard the Israelis were looking for a journalist who is travelling to Egypt. A Briton or American. I do not know. Be cautious, my friend. Things are not good and you are a good friend.'

'OK. Shukran rafik.'

'I will ring again if I hear anything.'

A week later David Holden, a special Middle East correspondent for the London *Sunday Times*, was found in a Cairo suburb shot in the back. He had travelled from Amman to Cairo after crossing from Jerusalem to Amman following Sadat's visit to Israel. There was no apparent motive for the killing.

There were other mysteries to come. Two Syrian Embassy officials were blown up in their parked car in Albemarle Street in London's West End.

Then the PLO's representative, Said Hammani, was shot to death by an Arab assassin in his office in Green Street, London.

The sense of violence was infectious.

None of it could be remotely connected with *Liberty* or with me. But I was still being harassed from other directions.

One of my friends received a call for me from a 'Jack Allen' who said he wanted to commission work from me for 'Newsday'. The only 'Newsday' I knew was a BBC Television current affairs programme. I rang the BBC in London and in Manchester and inquired if they had a reporter or a researcher called 'Jack Allen'. They hadn't and nobody else there had been trying to contact me.

'Jack Allen' had been asked for a return phone number and he had given one on the same local exchange as my friend who took the message. I passed on the information to Special Branch. An officer there rang the number and checked on the owners of the phone. It had nothing to do with any 'Jack Allen' or anybody remotely connected with journalism. The owner was a Derbyshire plumber.

The next day the lady who had taken the call for me, an old family friend, noticed a yellow Ford Cortina parked by the entrance to her driveway but not quite in front of it. She went outside to take the number but before she could the car took off at high speed. She said the driver had seen her through his rear-view mirror. She thought there was another man in the front passenger seat. The number was hard to get because the car was filthy and the plate had been liberally covered over with mud. She said it looked almost as if it had been smeared with dirt to purposely obscure the number. The same day Tito Howard rang from Florida asking where I was and asking for a contact number for me. It was 'urgent' he get hold of me.

For almost two years now I had been besieged by strange callers, had observed men in cars sitting outside places I occasionally visited, and had been harassed in many subtle but effective ways, for instance the flat burglary and the FBI trouble in South Dakota. My connection with Tito Howard weaving in and out of my often stumbling attempts to investigate *Liberty* had probably inspired many of them. I knew that I was listed in the FBI file on Howard as a friend and associate. What that implied I did not know.

A week after the last strange phone call I received another. The man refused to leave a return number. He would ring again that night at seven. I took the call cautiously and more than a little fearfully. The man said his name was Philip Bush. He was the representative of an American publishing house interested in the *Liberty* book. He understood I was behind in my contract with Quartet.

'From who and where do you understand that?' I asked.

In the trade, he said.

It was possible. OK, I said.

'Well, sir. You're so far behind you're in breach of contract. We could offer you a better deal. A straight fee of $25,000 for the material you have. No need to even finish the book.'

'What about royalties?'

'We prefer to buy the book outright and work on it as part of a big Middle East project we're doing.'

'No deal. $25,000 would be a stupid sell-out.'

'How much would you want?'

'$250,000 cash.'

'That's impossible.'

'No deal then.'

'Hold on. What about $50,000?'

172

'$250,000. No deal on less.'

'We'll pay you $150,000 US cash wherever you want it.'

'I'll think about it. Can you leave a return number?'

'I don't have one right now. How long do you need to think about it?'

'Forty-eight hours.'

'I'll ring you at seven on Thursday for a reply.'

I had already decided 'Jack Allen' was probably 'Jack Burnyar' of earlier calls, but who was Philip Bush? He could represent a number of possible agencies.

The Sadat peace initiative was bogging down. Menachem Begin's government was under increasing pressure from the Carter Administration to adopt a less intransigent attitude towards a peace settlement and the illegal occupation of territory captured in the 1967 war. Any published accounts of Israeli hostility and intransigence towards the United States would only further damage the already badly-flawed pro-Israeli sympathies of the general public in America, particularly the Jewish community. And Israel relied so much on American Jews for financial support.

I was aware that a strong anti-Israel movement was gathering force in the United States. In August I had met with the Vice President of one of New York's biggest finance houses, who had shown detailed knowledge of a story I had been investigating concerning a Jewish politician allegedly involved in a big bribery scandal and drugs cover-up with Middle Eastern connections. The fact that the man was Jewish was coincidental, but the banker made it an important issue. He said he represented 'a faction trying to negate the power of the American Jewish political lobby' and they were looking for ways to 'discredit' certain influential members of it. If I was having trouble with my investigation and needed backing for it, this could be arranged. The story could also be placed in an influential weekly journal which would pay well for it.

A check on the man's background in Washington showed he had clear and direct association with the CIA and now worked on a semi-contractual basis subcontracting the financial backing of certain CIA projects to the private business sector. This particular project in which he seemed to want to involve me was aimed at improving American financial and economic stability in the Middle

173

East by aiding a change of US political favour towards the Arabs and improving trade and business relations with the Arabs. The banker told me he understood I had good relations with some Arab governments and he knew that a consortium of US business interests, all non-Jewish, were prepared to pay well for introductions into difficult areas of the Arab world. He appeared to be suggesting an Armand Hammer exercise of culling business favour in the unlikeliest of places.

I suddenly realized that without any effort on my part there appeared to be many reasons why people should now show an interest in my work and contacts. *Liberty* was important. But, I supposed, because of my relationship with Tito Howard and his part in the Whitlam affair, it was natural enough for certain concerned business factions to think I was now some sort of Middle Eastern middleman, even if only by proxy.

When 'Bush' rang me back, I had rigged a tape recorder with a telephone mic jack.

'Have you thought about the deal?' he asked.

'Yes. I still want $250,000. I won't go below.'

There was a short silence.

'I'll have to ring back.' He paused and I heard him talking to someone in the room with him. 'Bush' had put his hand over the mouthpiece to muffle the conversation.

'OK. Two fifty grand cash. Leave your car parked near your old apartment in Redesdale Street at 2 p.m. tomorrow with half your notes and manuscript on the front seat. Go into the pub on the corner. Wait there ten minutes, then come out. Half the money will be under the front seat on the driver's side in dollar bills. Then repeat the exercise the next day at the same time and place.'

'Right.'

When he had hung up I rewound the cassette tape and switched the machine to playback. The only sound that came out was a high-pitched whine. I dialled the speaking clock with the record jack on. I played it back. There was a clear and perfect recording of the female voice chanting out the time. I telephoned a contact in the security business. His speciality is electronic devices.

'Easy,' he said. 'The chap at the other end pushed your call through a scrambler, specifically designed to prevent you recording him with a telephone mic. Hard luck.'

The same thing had happened on a number of occasions in Washington on calls to government agencies. So I was not surprised. My friend had just confirmed that my caller was a professional.

There were too many professionals. I was too involved in their strange world of intrigue and counter-intrigue. I had almost lost my fear of involvement with *Liberty* and related matters. Now it returned. My guts churned and my forehead prickled with a cold sweat.

I was alone. I had no one to confide in. No one would care anyway except my publishers and I had been avoiding them because I had real doubts that I could trust anyone, but mostly because I was behind with the work on the book. I rang my publisher and we discussed the problem.

I told Special Branch about the Redesdale Street drop and they agreed to set up a surveillance. I left my car as arranged with a package on the front seat but when I returned it was still there. The surveillance officers said no one had approached the car. 'It was probably a dummy run,' they said, 'and you have now almost certainly blown it and spooked them by hanging around with us.'

I expected another call from Philip Bush but it never came. There were no more calls, no more men in cars watching my friends and no approaches to my publishers. Perhaps it was the quiet before the storm. Time would tell.

When I had made the meeting with the financier in New York one of the subjects we had discussed as an indication of continuing collusion between US government agencies and Israel over the nuclear energy issue was the disappearance of a West German ship in 1968. The ship, the *Sheersburg*, was carrying nuclear raw materials. It disappeared between Antwerp and Genoa and reappeared three months later minus its 200 tonnes of enriched uranium, enough to make fifteen to twenty nuclear bombs, and its original crew. The Israelis denied any knowledge of the ship, its cargo or the whereabouts of its crew. A joint investigation by the intelligence services of West Germany and Italy quickly established that the original crew had been a group of Israeli agents and the *Sheersburg* had been diverted to Israel where her cargo was unloaded. The CIA conducted its own inquiries and came to

175

the same conclusion. Israel had taken the uranium for use in its plant at Dimona.

Quite coincidentally, the day my original *Penthouse* story on *Liberty* was published a story appeared in *Time* magazine claiming that Israeli fighters had pursued and tried to shoot down a US Air Force Blackbird reconnaissance aircraft over the Sinai Desert just before the October War. The American pilot had monitored a conversation between an Israeli Phantom pilot and his ground control in which the Israeli pilot had correctly identified the Blackbird as an American plane. 'It's an American Blackbird,' he said. 'What shall I do?' The reply came back: 'Shoot it down.' Between 1967 and 1973 the US Air Force had conducted frequent high-flight reconnaissances over Israeli territory to pinpoint missile sites. The Blackbird had been one of these. Having a faster climbing rate and a higher flight ceiling than a Phantom the American pilot was able to avoid being shot down. He took avoiding action immediately he picked up the Israeli conversation on his radio monitor.

Since the appearance of the original story in 1976 I had not seen a sequel to it but there had been a wire agency piece originated in Norway which claimed an Israeli agent, who was caught with a group of other Mossad people by the Norwegian police after killing an Arab waiter in mistake for Ali Hassan Salamah, the head of Black September, had confessed that Israel had hijacked the *Sheersburg* and her uranium cargo.

Norway's former chief prosecutor, Mr Haakon Wilker, confirmed in a press statement that the Israeli agent, Dan Aerbel, had told the Norwegian police about the *Sheersburg* operation as proof that he was a Mossad officer. He believed this would secure his release. Mr Wilker said that Aerbel indicated the *Sheersburg* operation had been conducted with the full approval of the CIA.

In 1977, the London Sunday *Observer* had published a detailed account of the *Sheersburg* story, based on the statement of Aerbel and the further statement confirming what Aerbel had told the Norwegian police by Mr Wilker. The trail stopped there. In an attempt to revive it I had tracked down to Paris an Israeli woman agent involved in the affair, believing she had left the service of Mossad; but French security agency contacts told me this was not so and I backed off.

On Sunday, 5 March 1978, the *Observer* ran a single column piece on its front page written by Ian Mather and top headed 'Israel did steal uranium ship'.

The story was based on the release the previous week of a document by the US Nuclear Regulatory Commission relating to theft of nuclear materials. It contained part of a statement by Mr Carl Duckett, head of science and technology at the CIA since 1967. This statement was classified and when asked about it the CIA had claimed its inclusion in the Regulatory Commission document was an error.

Duckett's statement said that in 1968 the CIA had evidence that Israeli agents had spirited away the *Sheersburg* and taken its uranium to Israel; that Israel possessed nuclear weapons and that CIA agents had observed Israeli bombers practising manoeuvres only useful in dropping nuclear payloads. This information had been given to President Johnson; but Johnson, on the advice of Walt Rostow, had told the CIA not to pass it on to either Defence Secretary Robert McNamara or Secretary of State Dean Rusk.

I am now sitting in a room of an old Tudor hotel in the Cotswolds trying to conclude a story which has yet to reach its real conclusion. I expect there will be repercussions, accusations and many verbal assaults when the book is finally published. It is almost spring now. It is warm enough to work with the windows open. It is only two more weeks to the opening of the trout fishing season. Which has nothing to do with the story but was a great incentive to finish it. Tito Howard is due to arrive in Paris any day for an 'urgent consultation' with me. What about I do not know and really feel I do not want to know. I was told a fortnight ago that one of the *Liberty* officers wants to write a book about the affair, and Captain McGonagle is still saying he will one day write his own account. I sometimes wonder what has happened to Harry Fischer. He had no part in *Liberty* but I feel he had a major character role by proxy. Tito Howard says he is alive and well in California, thinking of ways to recoup his fortunes.

The publication of this book is only halfway the end of my involvement with *Liberty*, I suppose. It is all part of the continuous movement of the Middle East political war. Because of the book I will go to many places and meet many people. That will be a whole new part to my story; my friend Peter Grant said it is like Topsy, it grows and grows. The unknown is the more frightening when you know there is fearful substance to it. I wish I could write 'Finished' on this manuscript and know it would be truly finished. But I cannot and it is not.

Glossary

AID	American Overseas Welfare Department
AIM	American Indian Movement
AP	Associated Press
CIA	Central Intelligence Agency
COI	British Central Office of Information
DIA	Defence Intelligence Agency
DST	French Security Service
FLOSY	Front for the Liberation of South Yemen
HMG	Her Majesty's Government (i.e. British Government)
IDF	Israeli Defence Forces
IIS	*see* Mossad
IRS	American Internal Revenue Service
JCS	Joint Chiefs of Staff
KGB	Russian State Security Service
MI6	British Secret Intelligence Service
MIT	Massachusetts Institute of Technology
Mossad	Israeli Intelligence Service
MTB	Motor Torpedo Boat
NATO	North Atlantic Treaty Organisation
NLF	National Liberation Front
NSA	National Security Agency
PLO	Palestine Liberation Organisation
SAS	Special Air Service
UAR	United Arab Republic
UPI	United Press International